CW00495539

Published, produced, and distributed by:

Library Partners Press
ZSR Library
Wake Forest University
1834 Wake Forest Road
Winston-Salem, North Carolina 27106

http://wwwlibrarypartnerspress.org

library partners press
a digital publishing imprint

The
Appalachian
Trail

History,
Humanity,
and Ecology

Robert A. Browne

FOREWARD TO THIS EDITION

I hiked the Appalachian Trail in 1974, when I was twenty-three. I had never been on the trail before, had only backpacked once for just a couple of days on the Pacific Crest Trail. That had been a comical disaster, with hordes of mosquitoes (little did I know that they bred in snow meltwater), a burned up sleeping bag and consequently a forced hike out across a shortcut that involved bushwacking through a steep canyon. When I started the climb up Amicola Falls to the start of the Trail at Springer Mountain. I didn't know about were guidebooks for the AT. In North Carolina I obtained the first edition of the AT Fact Book, which I have fondly kept, and used that to plot out my daily hikes to the safety of a shelter. I needed those shelters, which thankfully were mostly empty then since less than 50 people through hiked the trail that year (compared to more than a thousand now). Foreshadowing the minimalist trend among today's backpackers, I did not carry a tent, using only a poncho for the two nights I slept in the rain, or a stove, instead using canned Sterno. I had no mail drops, relying upon visits to country stores, eating half cooked macaroni and cheese every other night. I spent three nights in town. I hiked mostly alone, which was my preference. The exceptions were the occasional hiker who happened to be on the same schedule, and when a girlfriend joined me for a few days in Pennsylvania.

During the more than forty years since I hiked the trail, I've revisited it constantly. I've re-hiked much of the northern sections, mostly while I was a graduate student in Syracuse. I completed Vermont's Long Trail, from its junction with the AT to the Canadian border, reveling in the great northern forest. For the thirty six years that I've been an ecology professor at Wake Forest University, a major focus of my research has been on the Southern Appalachians, exploring the population genetics and ecology of flying squirrels, voles, deer mice, pygmy salamanders and flightless beetles found on the high peaks. Although, I've done research in more than 26 countries, from the Mediterranean basin to the Andes and Amazon and Galapagos Islands, my first love is the Appalachians. When I was thirteen I attended a boarding school on the western edge of the Catskills. The school had a dairy farm, extensive forests, creeks, gently rounded mountains, and a commanding view of the upper Delaware Valley. I was hooked for life.

While hiking I kept field notes and a journal, relying upon them to slowly put a book together. I found a small publisher and the book went through three small printings from 1980 - 1984 before the publisher went out of business. There is an unresolved paradox in wanting to complete the trail for its own sake and hence never registering my name on the hiker's rolls kept by the AT Conservancy, yet composing a book based on hiking it. Except for minor editorial corrections, the current book is the same as that first published in 1980.

There have been numerous changes in the trail in the last 40 years. The AT became a National Scenic Trail in 1972, acquiring enhanced protection, significant financing and additional resources from the National Park Service. Since 1974, perhaps one-third of the trail has been rerouted, eliminating long stretches of roads like those that traversed the Cumberland Valley in Pennsylvania and the New York Connecticut border. It's become a less arduous trail, following switchbacks rather than direct assaults up the slopes. With more footbridges across streams, re-routings around flooded beaver dams, more hostels and way stops, some of the wilderness aspects of the trail have been lost. Yet, recalling when waves washed over my head and the possibility of drowning while fording the Kennebec River before a ferry system was instituted, I can also appreciate the positive aspects of those alterations. Perhaps, the most significant change in the last forty years is the loss of solitude. The popularity of the AT has made it much more difficult to achieve. Alternately, the highlight for many hikers on the AT are the friendships and bonds forged with fellow hikers. As with many changes, the change in balance between solitude and companionship is not necessarily bad, just different. For those who have completed the Trail, and for many who have walked shorter sections, hiking the Appalachian Trail is counted as a highlight of one's life. It certainly has been for mine.

ACKNOWLEDGMENTS

Permission for reproduction of the following quotations is gratefully acknowledged:

Excerpts from The American Wilderness: *The Southern Appalachians* by Jerome Doolittle and the Editors of Time-Life Books, © 1975 Time Inc.

Excerpts from *The Southern Appalachians: A Wilderness Quest* by Charlton Ogburn, William Morrow and Company, Inc.

Excerpts from *Strangers in High Places* by Michael Frome, Doubleday and Company, Inc.

Carole Gibson aided in proofreading and offered encouragement throughout the book's genesis. I owe her many thanks.

I would like to thank David Cutting and William Hutchinson for bringing to my attention the correct spellings for a number of place names and especially for the correct version of the Shelton story.

CONTENTS

INTRODUCTION

The concept of a continuously marked trail along the crest of the Appalachian Mountains was first forwarded in 1921 by a Massachusetts native, Benton MacKay, in an article published in the *Journal of the American Institute of Architects.* At that time, the footpath's length from Georgia to Maine was envisioned as one thousand three hundred miles, but with scenic diversions and reroutes away from private land, the distance grew to more than two thousand miles. The first section of what was to be the Appalachian Trail was constructed in 1922 in Harriman State Park in New York. Although a portion of the Long Trail in Vermont and scattered trail sections elsewhere were incorporated into the new trail, it was not until fifteen years later, in 1937, that the final section in Maine was blazed.

Earl Schaffer of York, Pennsylvania, was the first person to complete the trail in a single year. For 123 days, from April 4 to August 5, 1948, he hiked from Mount Oglethorpe, which at that time was the southern terminus of the trail in Georgia, to Mount Katahdin, Maine. The hardships were greater then, with canvas and board rucksacks in place of today's aluminum and nylon, fewer shelters, unmarked trails, and canned rather than freeze-dried foods. To counter these drawbacks, there was one plus: long stretches of solitude.

The southern terminus of the trail was reluctantly moved from Mountt. Oglethorpe to Springer Mountain in 1958. The thirteen miles between the two peaks covered entirely private land, was degraded rapidly by litter, vandalism, and commercial development. To avoid further despoilment, Congress in 1968 passed the National Scenic Trails Act, which designated the Appalachian Trail in the East and the Pacific Crest Trail in the West as national trails. Previously, the organization of the trail entirely private, primarily through the Appalachian Trail Conference. With the 1968 act, the federal government assumed a more active role, providing funding for land acquisition and, as a last resort, exercisinge the power of land condemnation. This act is especially significant for the 850 miles of trail outside the public domain at the sufferance of private land owners. The ramifications of the NSTA enable progress to be made toward the ideal goal of an unbroken "greenway" stretching from Georgia to Maine. Unlike other hiking trails such as the Long Trail, which has as its motto "A Footpath in the Wilderness," the concept of the Appalachian Trail is to transect the rural Eastern United States, including the virgin forests of the Smokies, the craggy peaks of the White Mountains, the cow pastures of Pennsylvania, and the abandoned stagecoach roads of Connecticut. This combination of history, humanity, and nature are what give the Appalachian Trail its uniqueness and are emphasized throughout this book.

More than 50 percent of Americans, over one hundred twenty million people, live within a day's drive of the Appalachian Trail. There is something mystifying, almost magical in the Merliynian sense, in having a two-thousand-mile footpath in sight of the Empire State Building or within a stone's throw of a worker in a North Carolina tobacco field. Awaiting the seeker is the "adventure of a lifetime," as the title of trail author Edward Garvey's book implies, or it is the afternoon escape from the masonry canyons of the city or the sterility of the suburbs to sample nature's wares no matter what the season. Day use of all portions of the Appalachian Trail has been estimated at more than one million per year. Long-distance hikers constitute only a small fraction of trail usage. With end-to-enders, the fraction is reduced to almost minuscule. Since Earl Schaffer, fewer than three hundred have completed the trail's entire length in a single year. Meaning no detraction to the magnitude of day or weekend hikers, it is the minority of through-hikers for which the trail is envisioned, for they carry the spirit of the trail, be it only as a dream for those who bear responsibilities that prevent them from hiking its entire length.

Through-hikers are primarily young and, if not poor, certainly not affluent. Like Odysseus and his son Telemachus, they search for adventure and experience—most at an age at which they feel a need to sample life's wares. More than a few, start with the "veni, vidi, vici" frame of mind and can hardly wait to relate their accomplishments to the folks back home. Far, far more start than finish, enhancing the exclusiveness of the club. Yet who is to say who profits more: he who trudges day by day for two thousand miles, or he who walks as far as his heart desires? His sole criterion is to walk with the senses—with hands that feel, ears that hear, and eyes that see. For as the last entry in Henry David Thoreau's journal reads, "All this is perfectly distinct to the observant eye, and yet could easily pass unnoticed by most."

INITIATION
GEORGIA AND NORTH CAROLINA

"The mountains, John Muir once said,
are fountains not only of rivers and fertile soil,
but of men.
Therefore, shall we feel (as Muir did)
that in some sense we are all mountaineers
and going to the mountains is going home."
~Michael Frome, *Strangers in High Places*

Dawn. After flying into Chattanooga, Tennessee, then riding a bus for three hours, I spent last night in a frosty woodlot beside Highway 56 leading out of Chatsworth, Georgia. Georgia brings to mind Scarlett O'Hara, peaches, and poor, white crackers eking a living out of the red clay. The term cracker can be traced back to the original settlers of the state—the debtors and criminals of James Oglethorpe's colony. To "crack" in seventeenth-century English meant to break out of jail, and the escapees were called crackers. It was the thought of crackers and their propensity for violence that made my night a restless one.

Midmorning. How I love these mountains with their white-framed houses and freshly plowed adjoining gardens. While hitching to the approach trail at Amicalola Falls State Park, I listen to a man tell me about his ex-wives, his hate of the law, and stories of stills. When I come back to the mountains it is a reunion of self.

Afternoon. To reach the summit of Springer Mountain where the Appalachian Trail begins, one must first cover the eight miles of approach trail starting at Amicalola Falls. It is fitting that the Appalachian Trail begins and ends on a mountaintop. There are many reasons for hiking, but one of the most important is to be alone for an extended period. I am a student of the solitary. Aloneness is important to me in terms of creative and emotional stability. I find constructive thinking only in solitary thought. I can share thoughts with others, but their conceptions come only when I'm alone. Herman Hesse writes in *Gertrude* that "creativity isolates one and demands something that has to be subtracted from the enjoyment of life." I am not so much a man who enjoys solitude as I am one who believes that only when a person spends the majority of his time alone will he appreciate his fellow humans. At times, one has to withdraw from society in order to appreciate it. By society is meant not only man in general, but also the community of friends to which one belongs. When one withdraws, the pressure to keep one's ego high and the insistent burden to demonstrate one's success can be discarded. In solitude, one searches, questioning again his reasons for existence, his treatment of others. Most men need others and need to be needed, but withdrawal adds another dimension: peaceful reflection and an increased awareness of the events that constitute his life.

Evening. I have arrived at Springer Mountain, where the blue blazes of the approach trail yield to the white blazes of the Appalachian Trail. A bronze plaque erected in 1934 on the western edge of Springer commemorates the hiker who searches for wilderness. The change from the 1934 hiker to today's backpacker is astonishing. The plaque depicts a short-haired, clean-shaven man with a primitive rucksack, knee-high leather boots, a drooping hat, and a smile on his face. Today's hiker usually has long hair and facial hair. His (or occasionally her) equipment is a magnesium-frame nylon pack with freeze-dried food and a goose-down bag. The transition in thirty years has been incredible.

Over Springer Mt.'s foothills, as the sun sinks and the sky darkens, the last burst of the kaleidoscopic colors of the sunset takes place. Reds and purples, and then gold and orange, and all the colors that sunset watchers know so well that there is no need for detail. Every sunset has its own glory, seen through each man's eyes, and that glory cannot be justly conveyed. A lone star appears above the hillside, a lone light lies upon them. I feel as I did while visiting the Smokies a few years ago. I belong to the mountains; the mountains belong to me.

On the first night, I wake often, either to identify unknown sounds or to turn from side to side, experiencing what T. H. White calls "that thin but refreshing sleep."

There are signs that man once has used the land where the woods now grow. Rust-encrusted barbed wire connects rotted post to rotted post. Occasionally, a good-sized tree has grown around the wire. The trees on this ridge appear to be about seventy years old, mostly shade-tolerant hardwoods, with a few pines along the south facing subsidiary ridges. If one reconstructed the ridge's history, it would probably read as follows: prior to 1830, virgin forest; 1830-1870, selective cutting of the most valuable species such as walnut and yellow poplar; 1870, clear-cutting of any trees greater than three inches in diameter; 1871, burned, as evidenced by an occasional charred stump; 1871-1905, farmed, with yields decreasing each year; 1905-1970s, succession from old field to forest, with annuals yielding to shrubs, and then to pines, and finally to hardwoods.

I take lunch in a refuge from the rain, a stone shelter atop Blood Mountain, thirty miles by trail from Springer. Blood Mountain derives its name from the carnage that occurred on its flanks when the Creeks, invading Cherokee territory, met the defenders in battle. The fight raged over this peak and the appropriately named, nearby Slaughter Mountain nearby. A large number of arrowheads and spear points have been found on the saddle between the mountains, bearing testimony to the story.

In the understory of this area of Chattahoochee-Oconee National Forest can be found small white flowers called bloodroot, so named because of the color that pours forth from a cut on the root tuber. The Cherokees used this substance as an indelible dye. In rare places, the five broad leaves of the ginseng plant can also be seen. It was once much more common, but the root has been harvested almost to extinction, serving as a cash crop to the backwoods housewife. In Asia, the root is highly prized for medicinal purposes. In Chinese, sching seng, from which ginseng derives its name, means "little man," reflecting the shape of the taproot. A ban has been placed on export of the plant, allowing for a reprieve. On the forest floor, these plants—along with the violets, trilliums, and other wildflowers—grow and blossom now, before light and nutrients are dominated by the late-blooming, frost-fearing hardwoods. I consider it favorable that the trees have not yet put forth leaves, which block many of the best views of the mountain ranges. We are indeed blessed by the trees. During these chilly spring days, the sun warms us through the bare branches. In the summer, the shade will dissipate the heat of the sun.

A red-epaulette blackbird, one of the first migrants to return, stops on a nearby branch to sing his song: "My territory, stay away, unless you're a female ready to settle down."

Despite scientists' preoccupation with humanly applicable results, I find my appreciation of ecology ever increasing. I fully support efforts to cure cancer, improve bone transplants, and fight microbial diseases. But there is another side of life that can be summed up with a quote from Livy: "Without art, mankind is nothing." Ecology is an artful science, one that does not necessarily aim to advance mankind in material ways, but instead enriches human perception of the surroundings. In my opinion, it does little good to increase mankind's life span by two years if this advance is not accompanied by an improvement of life through greater understanding and rapport with the environment.

Similar traits seem to characterize the people I've met on the trail, at least the ones planning to hike the whole length. They want the "experience" of hiking the Appalachian Trail to add to their lists. They say quite proudly where they plan to go, "Mount Katahdin, Maine, AT all the way." Yet they sleep, eat, and contemplate in clumps. Only one young woman whom I met on Springer, seemed to have a similarity to my own ken: She came alone to spend a few days in the wilderness. I am a lover of mountains first, humans second.

Thunderstorms and lightning dominate the night. The Tesnatee shelter, erected by the Civilian Conservation Corps in the 1930s, has holes everywhere. Three young men from the Pree Ranch in Texas share the shelter with me. Their heavy packs include such luxury items for a hiker as a transistor radio, canned bacon, and even a bottle of Jack Daniels. Also with us are a couple from Enfield Center, New Hampshire. Byrne is in his late forties. He hiked the entire trail a few years ago. His new wife, Jill, could easily pass for a boy, though she's in her late twenties. With typical trail hospitality, the whiskey is shared and Jill and Byrne offer me a place to stay when I reach New Hampshire. The trail passes close to their country home.

In the afternoon, five white-tailed deer feed on the bottomland grass. They see me and begin to move up the slope, except for a hesitant spotted fawn. An antlered buck lowers his rack and pushes the fawn to safer cover.

Charlton Ogburn, in his 1975 book *The Southern Appalachians: A Wilderness Quest,* gives an excellent description of the forest composition found on a typical Southern mountain. He first describes the trees on a slope of moderate height, centrally located in the range.

"The dominant trees are likely to be Red and Chestnut Oaks, Red Maples, and Sourwood. Half a century ago American chestnut would have been among them. Trees in a subordinate role would include three Oaks—Scarlet, White, and Black—three Hickories—Pignut, Red, and Mockernut—Tulip tree, Mountain (Fraser) Magnolia, Eastern Hemlock, Cherry Birch, Black Tupelo, and Black Locust, while Flowering Dogwood and Witch-hazel would contribute to an understory. Mountain Laurel and Rosebay Rhododendron would probably make up a dense shrub layer, perhaps with Smooth Hydrangea, Flame Azalea and Buckberry. For vines, Virginia Creeper and Greenbrier could be expected, among herbs two of particular attractiveness, Galax and Trailing Arbutus.

"Now let us move around to a somewhat drier part of the slope—one that catches the strong southern or western sun. Tulip tree, Mountain Magnolia, Cherry Birch and Hemlock drop out, the more desiccating sunshine is not for them. The first three have wood pores distributed throughout it rather than concentrated in annular rings, and this seems to make for higher rate of transpiration. Scarlet, White and Black Oaks join Chestnut Oaks as dominants, replacing others which lapse to second rank.

"If we proceed in the direction we have taken to the still drier environment of the ridge—though not a high, dominating ridge that would draw a large share of bounty from passing rain clouds—we shall find that the forest canopy, already grown less dense than when we began, will thin out further. The dominants are now Scarlet Oak, with Chestnut Oak in second place, and four Pines: Shortleaf Yellow, Virginia, Pitch and Table Mountain. Scarlet Oak's leaves are deeply incised, thus reduced in expanse, and have a hard, glossy surface; in this they may resist drying sun and winds. In any event, experiments with seedlings have shown that both Scarlet and Chestnut Oaks, for unexplained reasons, make better growth in dry seasons than wet."

My first twenty-mile day, 20.6 to be exact, wasn't easy. My feet and back seem to be holding up pretty well, but I am definitely sore at the end of the day. Strange what fantasies one thinks of as he walks along, mostly about food. For me,

Pepsi and ice cream top the list. Maybe I can pick up both at Wesser.

Better than ocean waves, rolling plains, or desert cactus, more than any other view in the world, I like the scene that lies before me. Small farms, recognized by the greenest of pastures, lie in a valley surrounded by forested hilltops. Clouds reflect the sunset's colors over the peaks. It reminds me of the Catskills, as do most other mountain scenes. High views are the first cause of my mountain love. They offer information, inspiration, and exhilaration. Information on the progress of the seasons; inspiration in unbroken forests contrasting with patterned pastureland; and exhilaration simply in being in their midst.

One, two, and now three lights have appeared in my magical valley below. Seen from four thousand eight hundred feet on top of Tray Mountain, the valley looks like the Shire setting of J. R. R. Tolkien's stories about hobbits.

This morning, I let the rain fall on me with just a T-shirt and rain pants. It was cold then but not too bad now because the rain lasted for only an hour. There is at least one advantage to the rain and mist: The hiker cannot see ahead to the next hill and dread its climb.

Having hiked the nineteen miles to Bly Gap, it's good-bye Georgia, welcome North Carolina, because I'm camping on the state line. Unfortunately, there is no shelter and it looks as though it will rain tonight as it has throughout the day. In order to have the lightest pack possible and in keeping with Thoreau's dictum "Simplify. Simplify. Keep your accounts on a thumbnail," I have carried no tent. I've tried to make a shelter by draping my poncho on a fallen log, but I have doubts about its capabilities. Perhaps I have erred, but I believe that too much security dulls one's urge to discovery, like raindrops on a roof lulling sleepiness. There's a need for risks like hiking in the rain or sleeping in strange places. The same storm that drops rain onto the roof also brings lightning and thunder. One needs both, with the ideal a balance between the gentle rain of peacefulness and the lightning and thunder of inspiration.

Last night was bad. It rained, and my poncho did not hold up well. I have slept most of the night wet and cold, but now the weather has changed. The sun has come out an hour after dawn, just in time for a magnificent view of the peaks and forests below, where clouds are travelers that explore the valleys between the hills.

There would certainly be a difference between choosing to hike this trail and being forced to hike it. If I were forced, I would hate every step, but by choosing I can overlook the wet nights and sore muscles for the benefit of solitude in the wilderness. I do not have any regret living in the present age. If I had lived two hundred or one hundred years ago, I would probably have been a hog farmer in the flatlands of western Ohio and would never have seen the mountains.

From the fire tower atop mile-high Albert Mountain, I can see my camp below and the line of ridges I have crossed. Inside the tower room are the bare essentials: a steel bed, a desk, the sighting instrument used to report fires. A sitting table for fire spotting, a radio, and a half-opened bag of potato chips. The tower is occupied only during the fire season, from October until the end of April.

Sharing the shelter with me this evening are two pairs of men. One pair are from northern Virginia. They hope to make it home for haying in early June. The other pair have met on the trail and hope to go all the way to Maine. One must be moving on sheer willpower because he has blisters the size of half dollars on both heels.

Every shelter has inhabitants of mice. Some are quite bold and begin scurrying up and down the walls, checking out the humans with every hesitant step, even before dark sets in. As I lie watching the burning embers, a deer mouse passes not more than three inches from my nose. Packs must be tied up at night; otherwise, the mice will sample and spoil the contents. One often wakes at night to shake the mice off his sleeping bag.

Each shelter is different; each has its own characteristics. Some are log shelters built during the Depression, such as the one tonight at Cold Spring and the one at Tesnatee. The newest are simple A-frames with one end left open. Some have wood floors, some dirt. Some are perched on hilltops, a grand vista extending from the shelter's front area. Others are nestled in hollows, a brook singing its song nearby. Whatever the style or setting, each is small enough to grasp immediately as home for the night.

A great horned owl calls in the distance, "Whoo, hoo-hoo, whoo, whoo." Owl pellets, bundles of hair and bone that are coughed up through the throat can occasionally be found on the field paths. To the Greeks, the owl is the symbol of wisdom, yet owls can hardly be called intelligent if that means the ability to learn. Owls are quite incapable of learning, with almost all their actions being innate. The great horned owl is the first of the northern birds to lay its eggs. In the bitter winds and snowstorms of February, the eggs are incubated by both the male and female. By now, the fluffy owlets are begging constantly for pieces of rabbit, mice, or, best of all, skunk. The great horned owl is one of the few predators of skunk, seemingly impervious to its odiferous characteristics.

In the early morning, the rhododendron wilts with the frost, as though hiding from the cold, but rises to face the day as soon as the sun's warmth touches it. A startling transition occurred this morning when the trail dropped from four thousand five hundred feet to one thousand seven hundred feet at Wesser, changing from inch-high frost to springtime beauty. Trees wear green leaves, lilacs and daffodils are in bloom, bees buzz about the apple blossoms. Houses are seen again, mountain houses with wood-slat roofs and rocking chairs on the front porch, right next to the 1940s vintage Coke thermometer.

I like to think of spring and fall as the seasons of change, winter and summer as days of status quo. During the seasons of change, the air is clear and bright. The colors are on the move: the carousel of autumn leaves, the living lacework of springtime greens. Spring and fall, although antitheses of each other, are similar, with color, clarity, and transformation as the common unifiers. Spring and fall are preparations for the peak seasons to follow. Fall prepares the plants and animals for the silence of cold winter. Spring serves as the introduction to the living zenith attained in summer.

A nice break at Wesser for lunch—hamburgers and ham sandwiches, even Pepsi at last. The climb from Wesser is hard. What many claim is the worst part of the entire Appalachian Trail is between Wesser and the Great Smoky Mountains National Park. There are no switchbacks, and the trail seems to go straight up. The only consolation about each hard climb is that it is behind you forever. Tonight, it is nice to be at the shelter with a fire to ward off the chill. I'm looking forward to the end of the cold weather and permanent springtime.

This is the land of the Cherokees, the people of Sequoya, a tribal leader who invented the Indian alphabet; a people who adopted the Constitution and bylaws of the emulated white men, only to have their land viciously stolen by their mentors. In 1838, President Andrew Jackson, who hated Indians since his fights with the Seminoles in Florida, gave the orders to gather the Cherokees out of their Appalachian homeland and march them to the deserted wastelands of Oklahoma. Sixteen thousand were driven out, with a quarter dying on that Trail of Tears, but a few avoided the roundup and sought refuge in the mountain wilds. Because it was illegal for Indians to own land, a sympathetic Indian agent, W. H. Thomas, amassed land holdings for the refugees via their savings and his own generosity. After his death, the Qualla Boundary was established, to evolve in the early part of the twentieth century into the Cherokee Indian Reservation.

William Bartram, a colonial botanist, was among the first Europeans to visit the Cherokee tribes. A peaceful Quaker from Philadelphia, he spent a good portion of his life roaming the southern Appalachians in search of novel and exotic plants. He explored where hardly any white men had gone before—along the tributaries of the Little Tanase (Tennessee)

River. His major work, *The Travels of William Bartram,* not only relates his adventures but also describes his twenty discoveries of species, including the diminutive Saint John's wort and the diamond-backed rattlesnake. Proceeding with total disregard for his personal safety, the Cherokees believed him to be partly insane and hence sacred, which may be the reason he survived to a ripe old age.

The eighth day was definitely a bad one, having covered the fourteen miles to Cable Gap Lean-to in about seven hours. What is worse is the bad cold that makes my body feel like it has been put through a washer wringer. There was only one way to face the day: by placing one foot in front of the other and then repeating. The angles between some of the hills were forty-five to sixty degrees, with ungraded trail.

Last night was a recovery. Ten hours of sleep seems to have helped the cold. Right now, I am in Fontana doing laundry and restocking food. Despite its billing as "the Smokies' largest resort," Fontana Village has all the appearance and charm of an army post, which is not surprising because it was built under government contract in 1933 to house the workers constructing Fontana Dam, one of the first in the Tennessee Valley Authority system. I don't agree with all that the TVA does or stands for, but its service of providing free hot showers to hikers is not only commendable, but it also nearly confers sainthood.

THE GREAT SMOKY MOUNTAINS REVISITED
NORTH CAROLINA AND TENNESSEE

At winter's end,
a world of black and white
envelops the living dead.
hands that do not feel
ears that do not hear
eyes that do not see.
A tired corpse
worn out by a winter
that has lasted too long.
~RAB

On any one day, the hiker in the southern Appalachians, and especially in the Smokies, can encounter a multitude of botanical communities ranging from the agriculturally developed lowland coves to the near-alpine zones of the mountain peaks. The hiker can experience the vegetation equivalent of walking from Georgia to Canada within but a day's climb. For every one thousand feet of elevation gained, the temperature drops an average of two and a quarter degrees and the vegetation changes as though one were two hundred miles farther north. In addition, the elevation and microclimatic changes result in a rainfall gradient. As the moisture-laden winds encounter the high peaks, the air is forced to rise into the colder altitudes, where the water vapor condenses, resulting in rain. The high peaks, therefore, experience up to one hundred inches of rain per year, while the lowland areas may receive less than half that amount. These variations in elevation, climate, and rainfall, along with considerable differences in soil moisture and pH, light exposure, and slope orientation, have resulted in a botanical diversity that is difficult to match outside the tropics.

The Great Smokies is an ecological reservoir and has been designated an International Biome Reserve. Formed two hundred thirty million years ago, the Smokies were once among the tallest mountains on earth. Even now, of the forty-seven peaks above six thousand feet in the Eastern United States, sixteen are found in the Smokies, making it truly the backbone of the southern mountains. Despite its proximity to the early areas of colonial settlement, more than one-third of the park, two hundred thousand acres, is virgin forest. Within this relatively small living jewel grow one hundred sixty species of trees, more than there are in all of Europe. Many are the largest and oldest specimens known. More than one thousand kinds of shrubs flourish here, one thousand seven hundred species of fungi, 330 mosses and liverworts, and 1,230 forms of lichens. The diversification of the plants and animals found in the Smokies is a result of a combination of speciation through geographical isolation and a diversity of habitats, where elevations range from nine hundred feet to more than six thousand feet, resulting in a habitat spectrum from subtropical forest to almost arctic conditions. The habitats have been further compartmentalized by the mountain ranges. A prime example is the abundance of salamander species, with thirty-four found in the southeastern United States. Some are terrestrial, some aquatic, some breathe through lungs, others respire through their skin. They range in size from the diminutive pygmy and Cherokee salamanders, less than two inches long, to the giant foot-long hellbender, whose grotesque looks may account for its name.

Tonight, there are three of us sharing Mollies Ridge Shelter. Neither of the other men has been in the Smokies before. They plan to take a few side trips despite their hope to go all the way to Maine.

I'd like to be able to narrate an exquisitely transcendental encounter watching the sunset, but in reality the sun has set behind the mist well before reaching the horizon. Not every sunset in the wilderness is spectacular, but tonight's did possess its own quiet beauty.

> *Row upon row of charcoal ridges*
> *wrapped with everlasting,*
> *ever-changing wisp clouds.*
> *Light appears in the oncoming darkness,*
> *star holes in the void above.*
> *Sight into the night*
> *for the terrestrial inhabitants below.*
> ~RAB

Most of the night, Mollies Ridge shelter was visited by a striped skunk. It rummaged underneath the bottom bunks and around the fireplace looking for food scraps, going about its business single-mindedly despite flashlights and talk. How does one discourage a fully armed skunk from going about where it wants? Actually, it was harmless because the packs were hung on the walls and the three of us chose top bunks just in case such an uninvited visitor might arrive.

For the next fifty miles, the Appalachian Trail straddles the North Carolina-Tennessee state line, with one foot in each state. It is a good thing that there are no entry ports between states, or I would have been in customs lines hundreds of times.

Since reaching the Smokies, I have been crossing over balds, grassy tree-barren areas on the crests that range from garden to pasture size. Their creation is vague, but at least a few are recorded in pre-European lore. The Cherokees called them udawagunta. Fire and wind-chill factors are the most commonly cited originators, but they were almost surely enlarged through the grazing of livestock in the 1800s. I am sitting in the grass of Spence Field, one of the largest balds in the park. Unlike Gregory's Bald to the south, which is well known for its springtime displays of azaleas and rhododendrons, Spence Field is primarily a grassy bald with its four hundred open acres dominated by carpets of bald oat and autumn bent. I hate to see the sizes of the balds decreasing, but the forest has slowly been encroaching on all of them. With wildflowers spotting the grass and wide-open views of the woodlands, the balds are worth preserving.

Below Spence Field lies Cades Cove. This was where settlers lived in hand-hewn log cabins and raised bees, corn, cattle, and children in an odd mixture of folklore and ignorance. I'm glad to see the cove from afar, just as I've felt great joy by walking within it.

In the 1850s, Cades Cove supported 685 people in 132 families. Much more land must have been cleared then than the open areas of today's bottomland. Cades Cove had grown quite rapidly from its first settlement in 1819. Too rapidly, for the soil yielded less, and by 1865 the population had crashed to 275. Young men enlisted in the war or followed Horace Greeley's advice and headed west. The population increased again to 550 by the early 1900s, but then the park was formed and the cove emptied, lived in for but a century. Now only the fields, the old roads, and the log cabins remain.

The steeple of the Primitive Baptist Church and its concentric ring of graveyard stones serve as the focal points for the fields and forests of the cove. The church was founded in 1827, eight years after the first settler came to the cove. Many of the markers in the adjoining graveyard are just names carved on hillside stones. Perhaps for some, stone markers are all that show that they had ever lived, but I see their lives in the green fields cleared from the forest and in the hand-hewn logs of their cabins. That is a far superior monument to life than a granite marker. One stone in particular I liked read as follows:

Infant of J. M. and M. L. Rose
Born and Died April 8, 1885
Buded on Earth to Blom in Heaven

Another tombstone holds the remains of the discoverer of Gregory's Bald, near the Appalachian Trail on the southern side of the cove.

Russell Gregory 1793-1864
Killed by North Carolina Rebels

The story of Russell Gregory's death has been narrated by A. Randolph Shields, who lived in the cove as a child. A band of Confederates had set up camp near Gregory's cabin and "requisitioned" some of his livestock. All of this occurred unbeknownst to Gregory. Upon his return, he walked angrily toward the camp to demand payment. In the pro-Union cove, the sentry never thought twice about shooting an enraged mountaineer.

Beyond the churchyard, in the new forest on the fringes of the cove proper, beeches and especially pines predominate on land once used for growing corn. All four types of pines found in the Smokies grow there. Five needles in a cluster indicate white pine, the largest species. Pitch pines, which grow on the southern slopes, have three needles per cluster. Virginia pines, also called old field pines, have two needles per cluster and survive well in poor soil conditions. Table Mountain pine, also with two needles per cluster, is immediately recognizable by its massive cones.

Where there is adequate soil cover and water, the pines cannot normally outcompete the deciduous trees, but on the barren ridges, where the lack of topsoil allows little water to be held, the waxy cylindrical needles of the pines keep water loss to a minimum. Hot summer days, or the desiccation resulting from the combination of wind and frozen earth, quickly dehydrate the broad-leaf trees, but the tough, scaly pines hold on. In the Smokies, the pines flourish only on the dry ridges, unless fire sweeps the forest, in which case the quick-growing pines, with their light wind-spread seeds, are the first, along with pin cherry, to colonize the charred spaces, although the hardwoods eventually will replace them.

The trail now leads from new forest to virgin, with the undergrowth thinning dramatically. No longer do the pine and birch predominate, but yield instead to the climax hardwoods. The transition is from a multitude of saplings to interspaced giants. Why did the settlers spare these trees? They were old even when the first homesteader, John Oliver, came in 1819. Inaccessibility is the most likely cause. It also saved the high-peak virgin woodlands in the Smokies. There was no way to get the wood out profitably. Inaccessibility, I thank you. I am walking amid the ancient wise men of the forest. The Smokies hold the oldest and largest of the eastern hemlock, red spruce, yellow birch, yellow buckeye, yellow poplar, pin cherry, silver bell, serviceberry, and cucumber magnolia. The poplars are the tallest, the hemlocks the largest. If only the ancient trees could talk, as the Ent-trees do in Tolkien's works. Would they speak as sages, or would they tell only of their dislike of the cold winters and their intense fear of lightning?

Interspersed among the giants are tupelos, also called black gums. Because the heartwood of mature trees in this species often decays, they were used extensively as "bee gums" by the highlanders. The tree was cut, sawed into two- to three-foot sections, and taken back to the farm, where the sections were righted. A queen honeybee and a portion of worker bees were transferred to the hollow in the log. A flat board, capped by a heavy stone, was placed on top. In this way, the number of hives was expanded. Not only did the settlers obtain honey, which along with sorghum made up the principal sweeteners used in the cove, but the bees also increased the yield of the fruit trees and cultivated crops.

Back at Spence Field Shelter, it again seems to be overrun with skunks, which seem quite unafraid. The people who arrived here before me have been feeding them marshmallows and granola. What will happen in the winter when the handouts are gone and the little beggars have forgotten how to search for grubs, worms, and nuts? I accidently stepped on one in the twilight, but fortunately—how fortunately—the skunk held its spray.

Another nighttime walk, only this time to the bald near the shelter. I like to greet the night by looking for the first star. Above lie Ursa Major and Ursa Minor, fitting names in the Smokies, where five hundred to six hundred bears live. Cassiopeia lies just a little above the dippers. The Seven Sorrowful Sisters, better known as the Pleiades, twinkle their greeting to the hilltop stargazer. In the eastern quadrant, above Gregory's Bald, a shooting star slices the void, stringing liquid opal onto the black velvet.

The shelters in the Smokies are the homiest that I have yet encountered. They are spacious, with bunks for twelve to fourteen and a large living area next to an inside-the-shelter fireplace. The rock wall construction contributes sturdiness and security. This is a welcome change from the wooden slats and tin roofs of Georgia's shelters.

From the apex of Thunderhead, wave after wave of misty mountains lie before me, with Clingman's Dome rising above all else. This is where my heart belongs. I envy Horace Kephart, who lived just a short walk from here, near Bryson City. He was a librarian who came to the Smokies to leave behind his wife, alcoholism, and the mundane and to investigate firsthand the customs, folklore, and ways of living in the mountains. He knew these hills before they were parkland and wrote about the people who lived in the hollows up the creek sides. I envy his knowledge and freedom, both expressed so well in his book *Our Southern Highlanders*, but then it is hard to envy a man who's dead when you're alive.

Some wild boars rip up the forest floor with their tusks while searching for last year's acorns and grubs. The boars are the descendants of an original herd of fourteen imported from Europe in 1912 and stocked in a private game reserve on Hooper's Bald, located south of the Smokies on the Tennessee-North Carolina border. Although they sometimes attack if threatened, this group trots off after a few minutes have passed. Considered exotic ferals by the Park Service, the boars are destructive to the native habitat and plans are currently under discussion to eliminate them from the park.

Although occasional stands of fire cherry and yellow birch are encountered, the high peaks of the Smokies above five thousand feet are almost exclusively conifers, with red spruce and Fraser fir dominating the deciduous trees. The two conifers can be separated with only a little expertise. The spruce is larger, with needles that are green all over and the bark scaly. Fir needles, on the other hand, are green on top with white below, and the bark is smooth. Although the Fraser fir is the true balsam of the southern highlands, settlers knew both it and the red spruce as balsams. To differentiate between the two, the highlanders called the Fraser fir the he-fir and the red spruce the she-fir. Unfortunately, the Fraser fir population is on the decline because of the woolly aphid, a parasite that entered New England from Europe in the1930s and rapidly spread to the southeastern mountains, decimating the balsam forests. I'd like to believe, however, that the parasitism is but a phase in the cycle and that not all the Fraser firs will die.

Flitting about the fir branches is the not-so-shy Carolina junco, a close relative of the slate-colored junco. They appear so similar that only ornithologists can tell them apart. Both birds winter in the southern highlands but part ways come spring. The slate-colored juncos fly one thousand miles north to Canada to feed and breed, while the Carolina cousin flies but a few miles to the almost identical vegetation of the upper elevations of the Smokies.

Clingman's Dome is in the middle of a fog cloud. At six thousand six hundred feet, this is the highest point on the Appalachian Trail. The dome is named after Thomas Lanier

Clingman, a mining prospector who became a US senator and Confederate general, and who is also remembered for the ambition and vanity that matched the size of his namesake. The dome is a beautiful high country, near-alpine (Canadian) zone in Dixie. Fragrant Christmas-tree smells are caught in a matrix of fog drops, wisps of wetness streaming through the conifers. The wind travels with great velocity, telling any doubting souls that nature is powerful. The fog is strange, seemingly made up of particles of ice. It is a strange feeling to be on this peak of the world. One can only shout, "Yes! This is it. This is what is worthwhile."

There is but one sadness among the joys of visiting the Smokies: the regret that one doesn't live here. Now I sit alone but not quite lonely. How can one be lonely when he is in the mountains he loves?

Moonlessness (*The Climb Up*) Blackness is pierced by a star from the flashlight. Creek water can be heard running over the rocks but not seen. Sight is altered at night, for what is seen with a beam of flashlight is concentrated but limited and exclusive. A waterfall becomes a white drape of wetness. A tree becomes altered from a daylight symmetrical whole to a middle-night dual entity of a tangled mass of branches and a tubular trunk.

Moonsight (*The Descent*) As the batteries of the flashlight tire, the moon appears over the mountain horizon. It came later than I had calculated. Without its luminescence, I would have had to spend the night on the snow-covered peaks. The moon's light guides not only my steps, but also my eyes. Where before there had been only empty abyss, now appear the faces of the opposing peaks, so clear that even their stubbly beard of evergreens can be seen. The moonlight produces a change in the perception of the surroundings, which in turn produces a return to common reality. But even this reality has its deception. As I descend from the peaks to the lower part of the trail, the snow is left behind. Yet the moonlight seems to produce its own coating of paleness on the earth and its living things.

Walking through the Great Smokies reaffirms my belief in the beauty of the Eastern mountains over those of the spectacular West. I like the combination of gentleness and grandeur, and the harmonic contrast of the patchwork of forest and cutout farms. There's more to a mountain than elevation. The Rockies are much higher than the Eastern ranges, yet I find the Appalachians much more intriguing. The Appalachians are among the oldest places on earth. When the Rockies and Himalayas were but bumps on the plains, the Appalachians were towering above their present-day heights. From the Eastern peaks, one can watch life on the hillsides, both wild and human activity, yet still be quite a distance from them. What I like in the Eastern mountains is the very thing lacking in the Western mountains: watching signs of human life from afar.

The Smokies are beautiful mountains. I love only the Catskills more—not for their beauty, but for the memories because I know them best.

The path is occasionally dappled with patches of snow, like ice cream spilled from a giant cone. Despite the snow patches, left over from a late-spring storm a week ago, wildflowers bloom in profusion. An occasional trillium is encountered, mixed here and there with trout lilies, but primarily the forest floor is covered with carpets of spring beauties, which bloom so early they are sometimes called "good morning spring." The spring beauties are modest flowers really, but they grow in the woods surrounding a sleepy Northern town where I have lived and hence hold my affection.

According to author Jerome Doolittle, Newfound Gap offers a comparison between logged and virgin forest. "On the Tennessee side to the northwest the evergreen forest is still intact; the spruce and fir begin about 1000 feet below the ridge top trail and continue in an unbroken mantle of green to the summit. But on the slopes that drop away to the southeast, toward North Carolina and the industrialized and populated Piedmont areas, the valuable softwood trees have been cut down. In their stead are young deciduous trees. So long as they are undisturbed, spruce and fir cling successfully to their existence on these high slopes of the Appalachians; they flourish and replenish themselves with new seedlings. But when the trees are cut or blown down or burn away naturally, swift-growing fire cherry usually sprouts in their place, with a mass of spindly branches that elbow out most competition. Within twenty-five years the fire cherry grows up to forty feet tall; then it usually dies off—to be replaced with yellow birch, mountain ash and other slower-growing, but longer-lived deciduous trees."

Four miles north of Newfound Gap lies Charlie's Bunion, a granite outcropping perched a thousand feet above a forested canyon. It was so named because the outcropping resembled the huge bunion on the toe of Charlie, an early hiker in this region.

To the south, down the Boulevard Trail, lies Mount LeConte. At 6,593 feet, it is the third-highest peak in the park, a few feet below Clingman's Dome and Mount Guyot, but it does claim the distinction of the greatest vertical drop east of the Rockies. The tourist town of Gatlinburg lies a full mile below. LeConte is not so much a peak as an irregular plateau. Myrtle Peak, noted for its spectacular views of sunrises, lies on the eastern edge, while on the opposite end lies Cliff Top, equally noted for its sunset vantage point. LeConte differs from the rest of the high peaks of the Smokies; a lodge has operated on it for the past fifty years, and it can be reached only by foot or by horseback. The main building consists of a dining room and kitchen, while smaller log buildings hold the bunks, sleeping a total of fifty people. The water comes from the highest spring this side of the Mississippi. Perishable supplies for the lodge are brought up by horseback twice weekly, but most of the provisions are transferred by helicopter twice a year, fifteen tons at a time.

The park boundary lies about twenty miles beyond at Davenport Gap, where one of the branches of the French Broad River cuts through the Smokies on its way west to Knoxville to initiate the Tennessee. With more than eighty inches of rain falling on these mountains each year, the six hundred miles of streams within the park receive regular input, allowing for a rich aquatic fauna. Within the Smokies, more than seventy species of fish can be found, including the rare Appalachian trout, almost driven to extinction when sportsmen introduced the rainbow trout into its high-peak habitat.

THE SOUTHERN HIGHLANDS
TENNESSEE AND VIRGINIA

Sundown color clouds taken far with the wind,
time has been so far away, when will I begin?
I think of far-off places
and sunny starlight skies.
I wish that I could leave today,
but I've got so far to fly.
~RAB

Since I have returned to the country, each moment has renewed life, breath on the beach to a man drowning in the sea of civilization. The pace has slowed, but the base is broader and the love deeper. I would never return to the city. A man can as little do without sunset watching as he can be away from his beloved. I am as much ordained to watch the succession of meadow flowers as priests are chosen by God. Who else will notice the fireflies flashing their messages over the meadow grass? Who else will notice the milkweed seed tufts drifting in the wind like dreams drifting before sleep? Who else will watch the clouds pass over the moon at night?

Before dawn, blackness, like a quieting blanket, covers a distant lake. Above are the cold white individual lights of the stars; below, the cold white individual lights of a town. I am surrounded by black and white; that's all that exists.

The sun comes over the horizon, and the sky and the land renew their distinctions. The land is green and alive; small

37

clouds lie on top of the lakes. That is the most beautiful part. I never expect it to change, just suspend itself as it is. But the clouds dissolve, and I hike on till breakfast.

Once again, signs of spring are apparent. The brooks are refreshing, with fiddlehead ferns unfurling and dogwood petals strewn over the landscape. The white-bracted blossoms will yield in autumn to the red berries, which are the favorite food of deer, wild turkeys, and songbirds. Rich-blue violets bloom on the forest floor near the bracts of bunchberry. Despite their diminutive size, violets are patient, taking at least five years to produce their first flowers. They can live up to five years after that. Violets often reproduce asexually early in their life cycles or late in the summer via an easily overlooked miniature flower.

This evening at Groundhog Lean-to is the first time I'm not enjoying the people I'm with. Perhaps it's because I've expected to be alone in the post-Smokies section of the trail, but instead I round the shelter corner, just a few steps ahead of the rain, to find four people who stick to themselves, eating at a table without making room for a stranger. The couple are from Vermont, seemingly not very bright but extremely proud of their Long Trail patches. The two other men have just graduated from Georgia medical school and are allowing us to bask in their intelligence. Perhaps it is just as well to be cut off, for the solitude complements the raindrops on the roof.

The trail follows a dirt road for about four miles this morning. A white-haired farmer in faded blue-jean overalls plows a sloping field with the help of his mule. Since the 1930s, when there were more than two million in this country, the mule population has declined precipitously, the victim of mechanization and agricultural efficiency. Yet in the southern highlands, there can still be heard the shouts of "Gee" (go right) and "Haw" (go left). When dealing with mules, one has merely to remember the advice of Southern novelist William Faulkner. "It is a known fact," he wrote, "that a mule will labor ten years willingly and patiently for you for the privilege of kicking you once."

The old farmer told me that he was preparing the field for the planting of sorghum, which was imported from Eurasia in the 1800s when cane sugar was scarce. It is planted and tended like corn, but the tops of the stalks bear tall spikes of reddish seeds. Come autumn, the cane will be cut, gathered in bundles, and taken to a roller mill. A mule circling the mill furnishes the power to turn the cogged wheel that crushes the cane. The juice, at first light green in color, is poured into a shallow steel trough and slowly simmered. It must be stirred constantly and the greenish foam skimmed off. Paper hornets constantly hover near the trough but mean no harm. After simmering all day, the amber fluid is tasted for quality and then poured into mason jars.

Before the Revolutionary War, eastern Tennessee belonged to the Cherokees, with activity centered on four or five communities southeast and southwest of the Smokies. The Warrior Trail passed near here, crossing the upper reaches of the Clinch and Powell rivers, on its way to Kentucky.

According to the Treaty of Holston, proclaimed in 1792, no white man was to settle in the lands west of the Clinch. These were to be Indian lands forever. However, the state of North Carolina, which claimed all of Tennessee then, began to sell land tracts across the Clinch to Revolutionary War veterans. In January 1794, the federal government ordered the settlers out of the Clinch Valley for trespassing. But pressures for westward expansion were building. In 1798, the Cherokees were forced to sign the Treaty of Tellico, opening the area between the Clinch and Powell Rivers for settlement. All land to the west was thereafter to be Indian in perpetuity.

The hill-land economy after the revolution, but before the Civil War, centered on agricultural self-sustenance. Transportation was poor, and most crops stayed where they were produced. The Civil War divided not only the country but also the highlands. Most of the settlers were pro-Union, while the rest of the states of Tennessee and North Carolina were pro-slavery and pro-Confederate. There was talk of forming a loyalist state of East Tennessee in the same way West Virginia was established. No major battles took place in the highlands, but there were many skirmishes. Both armies used the area as a stopover. The countryside was ravaged by poachers, foragers, and numerous guerrillas, who fought more for personal profit than conviction.

For the first time, I've hiked alone all day without seeing anyone on the trail. Perhaps I left behind the crowd of through-hikers who set off from Springer before I did.

I passed through the town of Hot Springs, North Carolina, this morning, but not without replenishing supplies and eating an excellent breakfast of ham, eggs, pancakes, and coffee. During the mid-1800s, Hot Springs was a bustling health resort. During World War I, the town served as an internment camp for German prisoners of war. Today, it is just a sleepy farm town whose inhabitants are hospitable to Appalachian Trail hikers. Just outside the town flows the northern branch of the French Broad River. This river often serves for many species as the North-South demarcation line. Salamanders especially seem to hold this river sacred; Yankees above, Southern gentlemen below.

Part of the education and entertainment of long-distance hiking is in conversations with fellow hikers along the trail and over shared meals at the shelters. The journey on the Appalachian Trail seems to have a parallel in *The Canterbury Tales* of Geoffrey Chaucer. Despite the fact that the they were on a religious pilgrimage, they traveled many months, stopping each night to listen to various tales. Appalachian Trail hikers do likewise. Tonight, space is shared with two diverse women. The difference in their ages would point toward incompatibility, yet they have met as strangers and hiked together now for a week. The senior member of this pair is a grandmother type in her fifties who is attempting to hike the trail alone—or semialone. If the trail crosses a paved road, her husband meets her in their camper with a hot meal on the stove and a shower at the ready. Something gained, something lost in this plan, but considering Helen's age, I admire her willingness to walk despite this deviance from the end-to-ender's concept of wilderness purity. Helen's younger companion could pass in looks for the archetype of her profession, a librarian. She has been walking consecutive sections of the trail during her annual vacation leave each summer since her freshamn year of college.

This night was the coldest to date. At 6:30 a.m. this morning when I arose reluctantly, the temperature was twenty-six degrees. Hoar frost had accumulated on the hillsides, pushing spinnerets of water into frozen threads—some three to four inches high.

For most of the morning, the Appalachian Trail has followed a hillcrest that runs southwest to northeast. It is the easternmost ridgeline before extensive plains to the west. Below are expansive views with no intervening foothills. Further on the ridge, the trail passes the graves of a nephew and his uncle, John and David Shelton. They were from North Carolina but fought for the Union cause and were killed while returning to Cold Spring Mountain for a reunion with their families.

Today and tomorrow, the trail traverses mostly private land, though for the most part still forested. One travels through a pasture where a mare tends her foal. Old women ask where you're from, then, as quickly as it takes for the sun to move behind a cloud, begin to tell their life histories. They tell of aunts and uncles who would walk to town only twice a year for supplies and who now lie buried in the backwoods. They tell of their gardens, apple trees, and a favorite season.

Tonight, I'm traveling through a twenty-four-mile section where there are no shelters, so it is campout time. At least the weather is clear, but it will probably be as cold tonight as last night. As I lie in my sleeping bag waiting for sleep, a ruffed grouse approaches. Despite head movements on my part, the bird comes within five feet, clucking, strutting, and spreading its tail into a display. From my vantage, there is no female to watch this ostentatious male. Like the arctic owls, the ruffed grouse undergoes nine- to eleven-year density cycles, and, like the owl, the primary cause is thought to be the population cycles of its own food. Grouse do not migrate, but rather spend their summers here in the open woods and winters in the conifers.

At these elevations, I am still in the coniferous forest. Wood sorrel, looking like the shamrocks of old Ireland, share the role, along with the mosses, as the dominant covers of the fir forest floor. Rising above the mosses is an occasional winter-berry plant, commonly found in the three-thousand-foot range in the southern highlands. It is a close relative of the holly, but unlike that species, is deciduous, bearing only its bright-red berries through the snowfalls. This will be among the last stands of the coniferous forest until New York and New England.

A few miles later, the firs yield to stands of low-hanging, fragrant birch. Sweet and yellow birch are the two varieties that dominate in the southern highlands. Sweet birch has dark, smooth, cherry-like bark with glistening highlights where the sap has accumulated. The hardwood is prized by lumbermen for use in fine furniture and cabinetry, and its twigs are prized by the backwoods wanderer for their refreshing wintergreen taste. Yellow birch, on the other hand, is named after its bark, which peels into curly, thin, silvery-yellow strips. Its wood is heavy and strong but difficult to work, and hence is usually used for plywood and boxes.

Wildflowers carpet the forest floor, so thick that they look like snow upon the ground, so dense that the hum of pollinating bees sounds like the center of a hive. One of the bees, exhausted and close to death, rests on a flower. She has spent her sixty-day life for the hive, working herself to death, so that the queen may bear offspring that carry some of her genes.

Climbing Unaka Mountain seems like a desert trip. I'm getting the feel of the mountains so I can tell whether they have water on them or not. Lots of barren white rock and sparse vegetation cover hint at limited water supplies, but that warning does me little good because, for lightness' sake, I carry only a pint of water. The day is fairly hot, near 80 degrees, and my pint is gone halfway through the climb. It isn't until a few miles down that I come across a detritus-filled spring, but even that tea-colored water seems sent from heaven.

My home is the outdoors, not the space surrounded by the walls of a house. It is to nature that I come for warmth, for entertainment, and for involvement. I favor solitude. Even walking with one person who says next to nothing, speaking only after thought, is unfavorable compared with walking alone. The lone hiker sets his own pace, walking as fast or as slow as he wants. There is no clanging metal cup to disturb his thoughts, nor anyone in front to impair the view. Most of all, there is no one to interrupt a wandering mind. One harmonizes completely with nature. Singing is uninhibited. There is time to inspect wildflowers, grubs, and tree buds.

On Roan Mountain, many people gather ramps, wild members of the onion family, only with broader leaves. Southern hill folk consider them quite a delicacy, liking nothing better for dinner than spring ramps and bacon fat. Ramps thrive only above three thousand feet, making them strictly a mountain provision. In past years, the spring pilgrimage to the ramp patch marked the end of winter meals, which consisted only of dried or stored vegetables. The broadleaf, bulbous plants were dug up with a short-handled hoe and either tossed into a burlap sack or eaten with the day's packed lunch. The only ones to abstain were the young folks acourtin', for the garlic-like smell of uncooked ramps remains on the breath for several days.

The climb up Roan Mountain is steep—two thousand feet in less than two miles. The harder climbs offer a challenge and a feeling of accomplishment when the summit is achieved. The small repeated climbs are the tiring ones. This is another problem climb with regard to water. My pint is again empty well before the top. Although there is a state park on the summit, the water hasn't been turned on for the season. It is hard to conceive of now, with a cold spring gurgling only a few feet away, but dehydration becomes advanced enough to allow me to seriously consider toilet water for drinking. Now I know why shipwrecked sailors drink seawater knowing that it will kill them.

Roan Mountain, at 6,150 feet, has been popular since colonial times. Asa Gray, the famous botanist from Harvard, called it one of his favorite collecting areas, delighting especially in the heaths. In 1877, a former Union general built a log lodge with twenty rooms on the peak, but that was replaced in 1885 with the 166-room Cloudland Hotel. Today, nothing but a few foundation stones remain to mark the hotel's site.

With the ascent of Roan Mountain accomplished, there are no more peaks above six thousand feet until Mount Washington in New Hampshire. In fact, there are only a few peaks along Shenandoah and later in Vermont, where the elevation climbs above four thousand feet. This is good for the feet but bad for the elevation of spirit that the highlands provide.

The meadow voles are active an hour before sunset on the grassy balds. The voles can be differentiated from the other common mice by their tiny ears and short, furry tails. Like most otter rodents, their reproductive potential is high. The female can breed at twenty-five days and can bear young forty-five days after her own birth. The voles scurry in apparent panic so that five to ten can be seen at a time. They seem to ignore me as they come within two to three feet even when I move. The only explanation I can think of is that the juveniles, especially males, are being driven from their parents' territories, as happens with the closely related lemmings.

The trail crosses over a small dirt path in a mountain gap that John Sevier and his one thousand four hundred East Tennessee backwoods men used in October 1780 to travel to the site of the Battle of King's Mountain. The engagement wasn't much as far as men killed or territory won, but it checked the British advance in the southern theater and played an important role in the outcome of the revolution.

Lord Cornwallis surrendered at Yorktown almost exactly one year after the battle. Sevier became president of Franklin, the independent predecessor to the state of Tennessee, and later served as the state's first governor. The county that includes Clingman's Dome and Gatlinburg is named after Sevier because he lived a good portion of his life in that region just outside the Smokies.

Coming out of the forest and onto cultivated lands, I met a weather-worn man planting potatoes. Dan Winter told me that his great-grandfather used to own all these lands, including Big Hump Bald. He sold Big Hump, about twenty thousand acres, for a pair of horseshoes when the land started to be taxed. Dan is building a home near Big Cave, on the edge of Big Hump, to retire to and says that someday he would like to hike the length of the trail. For a man who's in his sixties and has spent most of his life within five miles of the place of his birth, I think that idea will remain more of a dream than an actuality.

Past Big Hump, the trail passes beautiful orchards—row upon row of apple trees in velvet white blooms. A few of the blossoms have transformed into the tiny ovules that will be the nuclei of the autumn's fruit. Apple trees were important crops to the first settlers. Soon after a homestead was cleared, apple trees were planted. The fruit was eaten raw, made into pies with sorghum, or dried for use in the winter. Today, the smell of the trees is intoxicating, both to me and the numerous honeybees that visit the flowers.

The Laurel Falls section may be the most harmonic area that the trail has gone through. There are no awesome views as there have been. Instead, the trail follows an abandoned railroad bed constructed in 1924 and 1925 during logging of the gorge. The tracks and ties are gone, but the bed still winds between sheer rock cuts. Over the passes may be seen magnificent views of the river, five hundred feet below. The crown jewel is Laurel Falls, where white froth rushes over jumbled black rocks. The water falls over a rock wall so steep that only a few rhododendron find a tenacious foothold. This rhododendron is the first I have seen in bloom. The flowers are light pink-purple, covering most of the plant. It might be *Rhododendron calibrese,* which is relatively rare except at high altitudes such as Roan Mountain, but is more likely the much commoner *Rhododendron catawba.* The flowers of the closely related laurel plant, known locally as ivy, have white pentagon-pointed shapes about an inch in diameter with scarlet highlights, and can be distinguished from rhododendron by the thinner, smaller leaves. Rhododendron, mountain laurel, and azaleas, along with blueberry, huckleberry, male berry, and wintergreen, are the component members of the Ericaceae, the heath family (named after the unrelated Scottish heather). In the southern Appalachians, the heaths reach the peak of their development, occurring singly as an understory plant, or in massive impenetrable stands, called "slicks" by the highlanders because of the shiny, smooth leaves.

A lone crow circles the summits as I bathe in Laurel Falls—my first bath outside on the trail—swimming in April, in frigid, invigorating water.

A scarlet tanager sings from a tree branch overhanging a cliff in front of Vanderventer Lean To Its exotic plumage attests to the tropical heritage of the scarlet tanager. The female is but a dull yellow below and olive green above, but the male has rich red feathers with velvet black wings and tail. The male probably pays a higher predatory price for his flashy attire because it is shed for the muted colors of the female as soon as the breeding season has ended in late July or August. The singer's perch overlooks neat farm fields, undulating ribbons of forest, and Watauga Lake, two thousand feet below. Down there, the trees have fully leafed, but they have barely budded here on the heights.

A signature on the wall of the lean-to reads, "Chuck and Johnny Ebersole with Snuffy (beagle dog with pack). Appalachian Trail, Georgia to Maine, 136 days. 1964. 31 March—17 September." Chuck supposedly wrote an article in *National Geographic* about their trip, but I'm perplexed: If that is their signature, how did they know ahead of time their ending date?

A gray fox sits quietly on a fire road, appearing almost domestic, unaware of my presence. Smaller than his red cousin, who prefers open farmland, the more reclusive gray is found mostly in timbered swamp and brush. As summer approaches, the area he patrols is gradually shrinking from its wintertime high of a twenty-mile radius to the one- or two-mile radius of summer when food supplies are plentiful.

Today is foggy, making hiking less pleasurable because one feels closed in all day. The trail follows a high ridgeline, but there is no view. Yet overall, I've been more than fortunate—only two days of rain out of twenty-one.

A little lower and I'm no longer looking down upon the clouds; rather, I'm in them. The clouds deposit water droplets on circular spider webs; the moist white diamonds surround this morning's jewel of color, a black and yellow wood spider. The dewdrops upon the wide grass leaves look like a glass ladybug herding over her spat of transparent children.

Just prior to Damascus, Virginia, the trail passes a grave marker, overgrown by forest, which reads as follows:

Uncle Nick Grindstaff
Born December 26, 1851
Died July 22, 1923
Lived alone, suffered alone, died alone.

According to most reports, Nick sought the solace of the high woods after he was beaten and robbed on a trip to the West. He had only one companion, a small dog, although his lower hillside neighbors would stop by occasionally. The last line of the marker tells the rest, except that when Nick's body was finally discovered, the dog was standing faithfully by it. It could never be tamed afterward and eventually had to be killed.

The last county in Tennessee that the trail traverses is named after General John Sullivan, who fought in the

Revolutionary War and then served in the Continental Congress and as president of New Hampshire. Sullivan County, New York, my boyhood home, is named after the same man.

The spirit of the trail is within me. I live on it and with it. Many other hikers frequently visit towns for overnight stays, but Damascus, Virginia, 425 miles from Springer Mountain, will be my first overnight stay, and that is mostly because it is the only way to obtain a shower.

Good-bye to Tennessee and North Carolina. Hello to one of the states I've lived in. I've felt something in the eleven miles to town this morning—not anxiety, but rather anticipation. Three warm meals, a clean body, fresh clothes, and a bed to sleep on—the basic pleasures of life so long taken for granted before this trip. If nothing else, this venture is worthwhile for noting and appreciating what I normally have. But there is so much more.

Entering Damascus is like a homecoming, with cattle bellowing their emotions. Apple trees are in full bloom with transparently milky blossoms. Cow pastures are mantled in light green, forests in darker green. Where else would I be reminded but my homeland, the Catskills and the Delaware Valley?

It is easy to understand why Mr. Mock would choose this valley, with its beautiful streams and surrounding steeply wooded knobs, to build his mill. It also seems like a Grimms fairy tale to learn that he fathered thirty-three children by three successive wives. What breaks the fantasy and what is difficult to comprehend is that he sold his homeland to a land baron who dealt in speculation and acquisition. The baron was named Igleburger, and he changed the town's name from the American heritage of Mock's Mill to the pseudoclassic snobbery of Damascus. Still, the town retains vintage small-town Americana to the forest-filled hiker.

Perhaps it would do all men good to climb a few hills and realize the beauty of a scene observed from afar. Even a small country town with its unkempt and sometimes deserted building shines like the valley's jewel when seen from the hilltops.

Now that the number of people on the trail has thinned, the hikers one does meet are considerably friendlier. Each stops to tell of what lies ahead and to relate any adventures. When there were many people, most just nodded and then walked on by. After Damascus, the trail has been frustrating, with detours to avoid private property. The shelter listed in the mileage fact book was either nonexistent or whisked away since the fact book's last printing. Tonight, I'll camp about thirteen miles north of Damascus.

The trail has been rerouted over Mount Rogers, at 5,729 feet the highest point in Virginia. It is named after New England geologist William Bartram Rogers but is commonly known locally as Big Balsam. The top-of-the-world beautiful balds are now left behind. Because there are no more five-thousand-foot mountains between here and New Hampshire, logic deems that it should be downhill all the way.

Since the Virginia border, the hills have become greener. However, I don't expect the ridges to be in complete bloom until after Shenandoah National Park at the Virginia-Maryland border. I don't know what to attribute Virginia's increase in greenery to—lower elevation or advancing time.

O Shenandoah, O Shenandoah
I long to hear you
and to see your restless waters.

The thing most missed, without considering physical comforts, has been intellectual stimulation. On the trail, reading is rare because of a shortage of good book shops or, for that matter, any book shops. Conversations with most hikers are too short to develop subjects. There are no textbooks to ponder, or newspapers or periodicals. For a month, their absence has been an enlightening change of viewpoint, but at Damascus a point was reached where intellectual stimulation was becoming as much a necessity as food and shelter (and sometimes a shower). I picked up Aleksandr Solzhenitsyn's *One Day in the Life of Ivan Denisovich.* The story follows a penal camp worker in Stalinist Russia for one day. Even in a work camp, happiness can be obtained if a favorable condition is compared with a less favorable one. For Ivan, happiness was an extra crust of bread, staying out of solitary, or the simple absence of pain. On a less-than-comparable basis, the same is true in the day of a long-distance hiker. Happiness is a bar of chocolate, hot water after ten days of dirt and infected blisters, or attaining the apex of a mountain, where the lungs stop hurting and the body stops sweating. The long-distance hiker differs from the prisoner in only one crucial aspect: He chooses his fate, while Ivan is forced. The book also contains an interesting poetic-image anecdote attributed to the Russian peasantry. They believed that the month's old moon was broken into pieces to replace the stars that had fallen.

When one has little reading material, he reads what he has slowly, making sure that the ideas forwarded by the author are thoroughly reviewed. One could make quite a case against speed reading because no time is allotted to review the ideas read.

The day has been grim since dawn. Rain and chill winds have been my companions. Walking has had but one goal—to get to the next shelter. Consequently, Killinger Creek LT, seventeen miles from the day's start, was reached by 1:00 p.m. There wasn't much to see in the foggy drizzle, although the redbuds were in bloom around Teas, Virginia. I also roused a couple of deer with their high-flashing white tails.

The shelters in Virginia are improvements over the Tennessee variety, which were constructed of concrete blocks with wire bunks inside. Very stark. Killinger Creek LT is typical of Virginia shelters. The entire structure is wood, with a raised floor for eating, sleeping, and general living space. It is not only more comfortable, but the wood also lends a home-like atmosphere.

After a morning in the rain, hot cocoa is loveliness to frigid hands and a wet body.

Virginia is the mother of states with seven formed out of her original boundaries. She might also prove to be the ideal state for the Appalachian Trail hiker, both in terms of time and physical stress. The trail follows primarily ridgetops, with few valleys to traverse, and hence exertion is kept to a minimum. The ridges also provide magnificent views of Piedmont plantation lands stretching to the east and the Shenandoah River Valley to the west. The trail travels through both farmland and deep forest, providing diversity when nature is at the height of her beauty, the glorious month of May. It is an area rich in heritage. The first settlers in America were Virginians. The state was the pivot point for the fates of two wars: the Revolutionary War and, fourscore years later, the Civil War. Her five hundred miles of trail hold great promise for anyone who cares to undertake them.

A wild turkey feeds on mast under an oak. With no warning, feathers explode out of the thicket and then transform into rapidly beating wings propelling the body into the safety of the forest ahead. For such a large bird, the speed of flight is amazing.

A few people have commented on my speed of travel, about eighteen to twenty miles per day, with apparent disapproval. Yet I stop to inspect anything of interest: flower or animal, forest-fire tower or abandoned house. The difference is only in how long one spends in the shelter playing cards, cooking, or sleeping. I still arrive by 5:00 p.m. or 6:00 p.m., allowing five hours to write, read, eat, and think.

The leaves of the mountain ash's buds are curled, almost like a rabbit's ear. The flowers are compound, with small ovules that look like berries in the middle. The mountain ash, despite its name, is not a true ash but rather belongs to the rose family. Later, its bright orange berries will add holiday color to the emerald woods.

Breakfast at Lookout Mountain, where both the Appalachian Trail and US 21 cross Walker Mountain. The restaurant-souvenir shop was built in the forties in the style of an English Tudor manor, with wooden beams and whitewashed walls dominating. I arrived before the 7:00 a.m. opening time and had to wait awhile, dreaming of hotcakes, coffee, and sausage. Being the only customer at this early hour, I ate with the family that lived upstairs. The two children had hot cereal and then it was off to school. Halfway through my dream breakfast turned into reality, a local trapper arrived to join us. He was quite interested in the area where the wild turkey was seen. According to him, turkeys can be trapped by building a pen with a low cross bar at the opening. Corn is spread around the entrance that the gobblers feed upon with their heads down, following the grain into the pen. When the corn in the cage is depleted, the turkeys straighten to look for an exit but never think to stoop down and escape the way they came in.

After our discussion about turkeys, the trapper and the proprietor struck a bargain. The trapper promised to deliver five to ten rattlesnakes, for which he would be paid five to eight dollars per snake. A good deal all around except for the snakes, which would be assigned to the pit, a tourist attraction adjoining the restaurant.

A mile or two past Lookout Mountain, I encountered a man named Crockett who was collecting rocks and wildflowers. He gave lectures on the same subjects, like a modern-day William Bartram. Expressing his envy of the long-distance Appalachian Trail hiker, he explained that his health and age weren't good enough or he would make the trip. He was just one of many who stated his desire to hike the Appalachian Trail, but it's a long jump from the dream to actuality.

I wasn't through with people yet. Past my meeting with a rock collector, I met a search party looking for a twelve-year-old Boy Scout who had wandered away from his troop two days earlier. They gave me his description and asked me to keep a lookout.

Because the trail follows ridgelines in Virginia, drinking water from springs is scarce. Therefore, cisterns have been built near each of the shelters and are filled from the runoff from the shelter's roof. Usually this works fairly well; the water isn't exactly up to spring quality, but it sure beats hiking a mile down to the nearest brook and back up. However, last night's supply must have been polluted. I attempted to boil it, but perhaps not long enough. Today, I have an acute case of diarrhea, which not only causes severe discomfort because I have to stop every quarter-mile, but also presents a logistics problem—my toilet paper is almost gone.

The fire tower at High Rocks is barren inside, with only the fire-sighting circle, the corresponding map, a telephone, and an insulated stool for the ranger to sit on during lightning storms. (I'd still feel vulnerable, ground wire or no ground wire.) A firefighter's manual, from 1947, listed the annual pay for a full-time lookout as $1,900 and he was expected to help out in road or forest maintenance when not needed at the tower.

Walking down the fire roads, I've noticed that the pines grow along the roadsides but nowhere else in the surrounding forest. Pine seedlings, which aren't shade tolerant, can survive only in disturbed areas.

Today was a pleasant walk: a little farmland, a little forest, some tree-lined, grassy fire roads. It would have been much pleasanter had an unexpected reroute not come up. If one expects to hike only nineteen miles, an unexpected four more can seem like eternity. The anonymous reroute planner is cursed with every step. He couldn't possibly have a just reason for this impropriety (but in reality, the reasons are probably excellent).

Pearisburg was a gratifying experience, or perhaps I should say the gratification was in meeting one person who lived there: Charles Beausoleil, a Catholic priest and a generous man. A hiker traveling south had told me about a priest who put you up for as long as you wanted to stay, no strings attached. I had reservations about imposing, but the opportunity for a shower is almost impossible to pass up. I had no more than said hello on the phone when he replied, "Where are you? I'll pick you up in five minutes." After a hot meal, fresh clothes, and the prerequisite shower came good conversation, a commodity that is highly valued on the trail. Charles loves his God and acknowledges his dependence on him. He considers that dependence a healthy part of his humanity. Charles saw in hikers a number of possibilities. First, he could practice true charity by providing for those in need. Second, he could enjoy the company of one of the most diverse aggregations of people in America, a unique opportunity for a priest serving a rural, isolated parish. Finally, there was the aspect that Father Charles found most appealing: the chance to homogenize some of the parts of an increasingly fractionated culture. He encouraged the hikers to eat lunch with the senior citizens group that came each day to the parish center. It's not often that economic or age classes mix in America, and I was gratified to see a white-haired grandmother teaching the intricate patterns of a double-ring quilt to a long-haired lass who dropped out of Boston College to hike the Appalachian Trail. A bearded transient joins forces with a Rotary Club member from Pearisburg to paint the church. I was in Pearisburg for only the day, but Charles impressed me as a man of integrity and thought.

Charles mentioned that the New River, which runs through the town, is the oldest river on the continent. I would doubt this, especially if the Colorado River with its ancient bed is taken into account. Perhaps the New River is the oldest in the east. The river flows north, which is unusual for rivers in America. It calls to mind Robert Frost's poem *West Running Brook*, about a stream in his part of New Hampshire that deviates from the norm and flows west.

Stony Mountain Lookout is the first of what I hope will be many fire towers where only forest can be seen from all directions—no roads or buildings, just trees.

The two-thousand-foot drop from ridgetop to valley stream seems like a drop from barrenness to the lush tropics.

From empty tree limbs and rock beds, one suddenly finds full leaves and blooming flowers. Lady slippers, one of one hundred forty species of North American orchids, grace the forest floor in profusion. Some of the American orchids are as showy as their exotic cousins, but most are rather retiring flowers that are known as orchids only to botanists. The showy pink lip of the Lady slipper is actually a nectar-rich petal specialized for insect pollination.

The Pine Swamp Lean-to was built in memory of Robert Trimpi (1951-1969), who was killed in Vietnam. At first, I thought that a more fitting memorial might be one dedicated to peace rather than a wartime casualty. Hikers are peaceful people, nonviolent to the extreme. I imagined that most would not have fought in Vietnam, even if forced. Now, I think that the evaluation was rash. It was a different era, and the majority believed that we were in Southeast Asia to stop the spread of communism into a country that was trying to defend itself. Robert Trimpi was a hiker and perhaps even considered himself nonviolent. He went to perform what he saw as his duty and died at eighteen. A shelter in the wilderness is a fitting memorial. Would that I have such a tombstone.

Azaleas are abloom in orange, off-white, lavender, and flame. They bring forth memories of finely dressed and perfumed ladies at dances and warm nighttime intimacies—intimacies that I miss.

Many box turtles are often seen ambling in their self-appointed ways near the trail. This fellow has the bright-red eyes of the male (the female's eyes are dark reddish or brown). His bottom shell plastron is also curved inward, a neat little anatomical trick that allows him to mount the female and therefore continue the species. Like humans, box turtles are not fully grown until about twenty years old, and may live to be eighty. Backpackers have much in common with box turtles. Both carry their homes, their protection, on their backs. Both proceed slowly, but surely, ambling forward with awkward gait.

Mistletoe is abundant in the crowns of the oak trees lining the ridges. Mistletoe is a true parasite, drawing nourishment from its host. However, during the barren winter months its evergreen leaves and white berries add color to a world of black and white. A red fox dashes across a logging road, not more than a few feet from me. With his (or her) mottled, soggy coat, Renyard looks as uncomfortable in the rain as I do.

Nothing soothes the wetness and cold of rain walking as singing—songs written by others, spur-of-the-moment songs, songs about times spent with another in what seems so long ago.

This morning, the view from the ledges of Tinker Cliffs are superb, overlooking a straight drop of two thousand feet. All is woodland below save for two houses, detectable only by their rock chimneys and red metal roofs rising above the forest canopy. Near here, Annie Dillard lived for two years recording her thoughts in *Pilgrim at Tinker Creek*.

Green spheres, about the size of ping-pong balls, have dotted the trail for the past two days, blown down by the thunderstorms and high winds. Their outer coat is a moist, smooth surface with slightly raised red dots. Inside the sphere are fibers that connect an inner core to the outside coat. These oak galls are caused by tiny larvae that hatch from the eggs of the gallfly. The larvae eat into the veins of leaves, secreting a glandular substance that causes the gall to form. The galls were at one time collected because of their rich source of tannin, valuable to the leather industry.

After thirty-three days alone, I'm glad to talk and especially listen to others. This evening is special after so long alone. The shelter is shared with five females: a mother and her daughter from Connecticut, who are out for a hundred-mile hike, and three young women from Cleveland who are hiking for a couple of weeks for a school project.

The trail descends from the Allegheny ridges, across the valley of Virginia, and onto the Blue Ridge—the long mountain chain that stretches south to just outside the Smokies and north to the Potomac.

THE BLUE RIDGE
VIRGINIA AND WEST VIRGINIA

He wanders, like a day-appearing dream,
Through the dim wilderness of the mind;
Through desert woods and tracts, which seem
Like ocean, homeless, boundless, unconfined.
~Fragment: *A Wanderer*
Percy Bysshe Shelly

Despite my general enthusiasm in hiking the Appalachian Trail, there are drawbacks: One feels degraded after living in the same clothes for seven to ten days with an unwashed body. The salt crusts on the T-shirt underarms. One is always hungry. Despite packing away close to five thousand calories a day, including a daily pound of candy, the craving for food is always present. At the end of the day, no matter whether fourteen or twenty-eight miles have been covered, the last two miles seem endless. The balls of the feet swell, and both feet seem encapsulated in pain. Hiking in the rain is always bad, but especially so if it is windy or cold and the trail is steep and slippery. All fourtogether are enough to call it quits. However, deprivation does have its rewards. On the return home, a pint of ice cream on a sunny day transforms all the above into only humorous memories.

Primitive men, especially those banded into highly organized tribes such as the American Indians or the village Africans, had manhood-training periods and rituals for adolescent males. Often, the boys were taken away from the village for a year or more and placed under the auspices of an elder. Circumcision or similar rituals were performed at the end of the training period. The trainees were then officially accepted into the company of men. Perhaps modern young men unknowingly subscribe to a rite of manhood: by entering the army, living on an island, pledging a fraternity, or hiking the Appalachian Trail.

The songs of the birds are becoming more dominant throughout the forest, both in the canopy and the understory. The whippoorwill ends the evening and begins the morning; seven or eight songs can be distinguished. All is quiet at midday, and then the pace accelerates again in the evening. The mixed conifer-deciduous forest that predominates along the ridgetops has been found to have the most varied bird population, of the eastern forests with an average of nine to twenty-two breeding pairs per five acres. Deciduous forests average ten to thirteen pairs on the same amount of land, and pure stands of conifers even fewer.

Just before the James River, the trail passes over Apple Orchard Mountain, so named because winds coming over the ridgeline prune the trees, giving the hilltop the neat appearance of a carefully tended orchard. Past Apple Orchard Mountain, the trail drops seven hundred feet to cross the James River. On its banks, near where the river empties into the Chesapeake Bay, white settlers established the first colony in North America. The climb out of the river valley is steeper than the descent, gaining three thousand feet in just a few miles.

Snowden, on the banks of the James, consists of a post office, general store, liquor store, and gas station, all of which are housed in a small frame building and managed by a man who seems to have time on his hands. Despite the fact that he has lived his whole life in the area, when I asked him whether Jamestown was located at the mouth of the James, he said he didn't think so. He hadn't heard of it. Yet the river was but a hundred feet from his door.

Mile point 697. One-third of the trail is behind, two-thirds ahead.

Near Big Bluff Fire Tower, a curious monument was erected in 1968 to inform the hiker that on this exact spot in 1891, the body of littlefour year old Ottie Cline Powel was found—seven miles from the schoolhouse from which she had wandered. I found it odd that seventy-seven years had passed before erecting a monument to a little girl's perseverance to live.

In Punch Bowl Pond, red-eft salamanderss swim among the water plants. I caught one female that had a swelling around her cloaca. Her underbelly was richly veined and swollen, indicating a gravid condition. Salamanders in a pond mean two things: First, there must not be any appreciable fish population because fish would have eaten the salamander eggs. Second, there will be few mosquitoes later in the season, because salamanders prey upon mosquito larvae.

Newts follow a strikingly different life-cycle pattern from most other amphibians. They lay eggs in the spring on the stems and leaves of pond plants. The larvae that hatch from the eggs are aquatic for the first three to four months before spending two to three years on land as red efts. They can often be seen brazenly walking the damp forest floor, safe thanks to the protection afforded by their skin toxins. The terrestrial stage is followed by metamorphosis into a broad-tailed, green-colored adult with red spots down the body. This form again returns to the pond. To make matters even more complicated, the newts sometimes skip the red-eft stage and spend the entire life cycle in the water.

On the pond's edge, bullfrogs call "chor-luck" and frogs chorus "peep-peep-peep." Answering calls seem to emanate from the dry woods, but perhaps they are only echoes. Bats glide gracefully and then suddenly swerve and dip to snatch their meals of insects on the wing. The pond water mirrors their movements on a field of dusky sky. Starlight reflected on the calm pond surface reminds one that he still has dreams. One's dreams are often his memories, just as the desires of the past are often incorporated into the actualities of the future. A man can be known by his memories and his dreams.

There is communication on the trail between hikers no matter how far apart they are. People ask you to give messages to their friends who are two weeks ahead. I inform people, either personally or through notes, of hazards or delights that they will encounter if they are southbound. In turn, I am the receptor of messages about unfit water, shelters that have good views, places to bathe, and snack shops and their contents, from people from the north who have already traversed what I am about to travel. Today, I talked with a middle-aged man who hiked the trail two years ago and made friends at that time with a man named Burt. As it turned out, Burt was one of the first people I had met on the trail. He, his wife, Jill, and I spent a rainy night at Tesnatee shelter. Hikers may be spread far apart, but there is some communication.

On the approach to the Tye River crossing, the fog has been thick all day. It's thicker on the mountaintops where everything—the plants, rocks, and me—are coated with moisture. The fog reminds me of the Olympic peninsula rain forest in Washington State; water drops from the leaves, but no rain falls.

North of the city of Roanoke, the trail parallels the Blue Ridge Parkway, an asphalt ribbon 469 miles long connecting the two largest national parks in the East: the Shenandoah and the Great Smoky Mountains.

Past the Tye River crossing on the parkway lies a crossover road called Cointer's Reckonin', a former tollway once used to haul mountain goods to "Gowhee" town folks and town goods to "Tuckahoo" (little potato) hill folks. Now the roads—toll roads from Indian paths, Indian paths from deer trails—have been eroded into uselessness.

The Germans were the first Europeans to settle the Virginia Appalachians. They migrated from Germany's Palatine via Pennsylvania down the Great Valley of the Blue Ridge, and they reached the New River around the time of the French and Indian Wars. Following the Germans in even greater numbers, and forming the bulk of the settlers, were the Scotch Irish, who, despite their name, were primarily Scottish, Welsh, and English, although most of the Scots came from northern Ireland, where the Crown had settled them. They were independent, God-fearing Presbyterians who worked industriously. The early settlers came with very little and hence depended on the first harvest for food. To save time, they did not clear forestland completely, but instead merely girdled the trees by removing an inch-wide strip of bark from around their trunks. They planted corn in the resultant shadeless areas under the dead trees. Later, they burned the trees and cleared the stumps. Eventually, they constructed rock walls and split fences, adding charm to even a dingy homestead.

The Southern Appalachian settlers built three distinct types of fences, although almost all were made from split chestnut rails. Most common, because of ease of construction, was the snake, where settlers laid down rails on top of a guiding "worm" pattern. Post and rail construction required more skill but less material. Least common and least durable was that of butt construction, where a single rail was placed on a pair of crossed rails, with subsequent pairs placed midway up the trailing length.

Shenandoah National Park, authorized in 1926, was the first national park of any significant size in the East. Its formation displaced 465 families, most onto nearby land. The poverty of the soil and the resultant poverty of the farmers were reflected in an average yearly cash income of only 125 dollars. The park still has signs of former human habitation. Rock walls tell stories of sweat spent in clearing endless rocks from the fields. Now the trees reinvade their former site. Occasionally, when I walk through solid woods, an encounter with an apple tree surprises me—a little more gnarled, fewer apples, but still a fruit yielder despite more than forty years left unpruned. A rot-resistant chestnut stump bears marks of a girdling. This glen had been forest, forest lost and corn sowed, and then forest regained.

The chestnut, with its cascades of white blossoms crowning the treetops in spring, was the end product of the Eastern climax forest. Now only bleached skeletons remain. Importers of Chinese chestnut trees accidentally brought a fungus into New York City that spread rapidly throughout the entire East in the 1930s and 1940s. The fungus penetrates the tree through any small wound, from there infecting the cambium layer of the bark, stopping the flow of sap, and literally strangling the tree. The Indians and their replacements, the early settlers, both valued the chestnut. The nuts, along with acorns, were principal wintertime-food components, eaten roasted, boiled, or ground into a paste and baked into bread. The settlers prized not only the nuts for food, but also the rot-resistant wood for construction of their cabins, shingles for the roofs, and rails for the fences. The chestnut also offered two cash crops for the highlanders, who were always shy of hard money: the tannin-rich bark and the nuts could be collected and sold.

A barn stands on the ridgecrest, its outer skin of sideboards removed, perhaps long ago, by scavenging homesteaders, or perhaps not so long ago, for firewood. The fields are separated by an occasional fencepost, still holding on to its burden of barbed wire despite the passage of at least forty years. Even the heaths speak of man, at least indirectly, for it was his sheep grazing— along with a short, harsh growing season—that caused the slope's matching woolliness. In the 1800s, overcrowding of the Scottish, Irish, and Welsh immigrants necessitated the cultivation or grazing of almost all of these mountainsides and hilltops. Today, only the valleys are cleared. It is better this way, for mountains were never meant to be cultivated. They respond with flash floods, silted rivers, lost topsoil, and barren slopes—quite a loss when compared with the norm of stable watersheds and beautiful, diverse forests.

The dandelions and buttercups in the mountain meadows reflect both today's weather and my mood.

Multitudes of dandelions
are meadow fairies
with halos of particled light,
dancing round their heads.
~RAB

The deer are again appearing after a two-week absence. They are brazen here in the park, coming to feed in front of the shelter despite the fire. This may be a result of the no-hunting laws, but the deer's scrawniness is probably a result of those same laws. With no predators or hunting, deer are not at all timid, but with the absence of hunting deer starvation is the flip side of the coin.

The coals of the fire have produced mystic thoughts for countless men through countless times.

Life without immortality
is like sparks from a fire drifting in the wind.
They are born in the flame,
rise with the heat,and are gone.
~RAB

By keeping a journal, am I striving for a piece of immortality that I hope is for all of us but believe is for none?

Misty clouds attempt to escape out of the valley before the first of the day's sun discovers and dissolves them. The hillsides, with squared-off pasturelands cut out of the forests, are brightly lit, but a sea of fog ebbs over the lowlands, leaving no   trace of town or house, of road or bridge. The fog clouds come before dawn and disappear with the heat of the midmorning sun.

Fog From Within:
Cobwebs of velvet whiteness
stretching from blackened columns of tree trunks

63

to patches of softened greenfog from afar,
mist clouds snagged on rugged rock peaks.
~RAB

The first shelter past Shenandoah National Park is the Mosby Lean-to. Nearby is the Sealock spring, named after one of the Gray Ghost's followers, Tom Sealock, who decided to settle on nearby land after the Civil War. In the close-by town of Linden, there is a mailbox that bears his name through his descendants.

The various hiking speeds and their names, with the aesthetic experience in opposition to the speed are as follows:

mountain time, 1.5.mph
wood time, 2.0 mph
ridge time, 2.5 mph
farm time, 3.0 mph
road time, 3.5 mph

The trail has degraded into twenty miles of road travel. Regretfully, I feel as though every year's passing will bring only despoilment to the Appalachian Trail. More people will hike. Solitude will be lost. Landowners will close their holdings, leading to despised road routes. This year, the shelters in Shenandoah National Park are closed for overnight camping, although the rule was not applied while I was there because of the off-season. How many more shelters will be closed or vandalized? There are good signs. A woman has donated ten acres so that a shelter may be kept. It's too bad that it is Memorial Day, because there are weekenders here, the first time I've been excluded from a shelter. Someday, hopefully, there may be an unbroken path of green stretching from Georgia to Maine, without any blacktop.

There is a definite hiker hierarchy, as structured as any Hindu caste system. On the crown is the Appalachian Trail hiker who is attempting to travel the entire trail. He or she is held in awe and respect, especially when the mileage traveled begins to loom large. Unfortunately, a few all-the-way hikers seem to be walking only for the awe that is accorded them on the trail and upon their return. Next on the ladder is the hiker who is traveling the entire trail in sections each year. The long-distance hiker is next. From here, the hierarchy declines rapidly: weekender hiker, day hiker, lowly tourists in suits and dresses, and finally, at the bottom of the well, Boy Scouts. If a hierarchy of hikers exists in the wilderness, perhaps no man is equal to others.

Good-bye to Virginia and more than five hundred miles of trail within its borders. Hello to the five miles of West Virginia. West Virginia has the highest mean elevation of any Eastern state. It is known as the most northern of the Southern states, the most southern of the Northern states, most eastern of the Western, and the most western of the Eastern states, but what I like the most is the state's motto, "Mountaineers are always free."

On the way to Harpers Ferry, the Appalachian Trail follows a former military road to the river crossing, passing the ruins of Confederate stone forts that were used for infantry protection. Not far from here, General Jubal Early fought his West Point classmates. Signal posts were built on these ridgetops to warn of North advancing on South or vice versa. Now South brings spring to the North. New Yorkers arrive not in infantry regiments but in camping battalions.

Harper's Ferry. Once before I had been here, but only fragments of that memory exist: stained glass windows that were portal lights in the rainy night, stone columns in the mist, bridges converging on a town that had passed away a hundred years ago. Today, the missing pieces from memories are transformed into the whole picture that is Harpers Ferry. The church with the stained glass windows, St. Peter's, sits above the town, halfway up the hill. Steps, hand carved into the solid rock 130 years ago, lead to the church and the upper section of town. No light issues from the windows tonight, but the church still seems to shepherd the houses below, just as it was a beacon in the foggy night on my last visit.

Although the mist and rain are missing on this visit, the streets are again deserted of crowds and tourists thanks to the twilight hour. Visions of the town lead the mind to return to the days of the nineteenth century. The town was bursting with pride over its position on the two rivers. Women swished in ankle-length dresses. Men wore felt top hats. Stores stocked penny candies and rich ice cream. Town folks nodded with respect as the master armorer entered his fancy house by the Federal Rifle Factory. Yet the town was soon to die, its demise tolled by the radical beliefs and actions of John Brown and his ardent followers. It was one of history's ironies that Colonel Robert E. Lee and Lieutenant J. E. B. Stuart captured Brown, who was later, executed. This town that straddled the line dividing slave and free states would itself be split apart and destroyed when the states divided militarily. Harpers Ferry was Union held, Confederate captured, Union burned, and then recaptured by the Confederates. The town's pride over its position on the rivers would be felt through four floods near the turn of the twentieth century. Harpers Ferry is in the past now, only buildings of a bygone age.

Above the town stands the viewpoint of Jefferson's Rock. Thomas Jefferson described the scene from this spot in grandiose terms: "A river searching for a hundred miles for a passage through the mountains, met by another river to split asunder the mountains and join with the other." The two rivers are the Potomac and its tributary, the Shenandoah. Jefferson said the view was "a trip worth crossing the Atlantic for."

A dollar and a half, plus a dollar for an introductory pass, buys a night in an American youth hostel. A shower, bed, and roof—not much more—but a good deal for the price. The people in the hostel are friendly, but after so many nights with all that space, a crowd seems out of place.

SOUTH MOUNTAIN
MARYLAND AND PENNSYLVANIA

Westron winde, when will thou blow
The smalle raine down can raine?
Christ, if my love wer in my armsis,
And I in my bed againe.
~Welsh Anon.

The trail passes through a number of historic areas in Maryland, the first of which is the Chesapeake & Ohio Canal, which follows along the Maryland side of the Potomac River. George Washington was one of the canal's original proponents. He envisioned a system of cheap transportation from the eastern counties to the mountains and even beyond to the Ohio Valley. The canal was excavated from 1828 to 1850, stretching from Washington, DC, to Cumberland, Maryland, still far short of the Ohio River goal. It flourished somewhat until a disastrous flood hit in the 1920s but never reached financial solvency because of competition from its more efficient rival, the Baltimore and Ohio Railroad. Today, the canal, where not filled in by dirt, consists of stagnant backwater pools. The towpath, however, has been converted into a pleasant walking and biking trail to the Georgetown neighborhood of Washington, DC.

A few miles past the C&O lies Gathland, erected as a memorial to Civil War correspondents. The donor, George Allen Townsend, was among this honored group with the pen name of Gath. If his memorial arch was designated as any indicator of his personality, then he bordered on the eccentric. The arch is inset with busts of snarling dog heads, words spelled out in brick letters, and quotes from the correspondents who have covered two thousand years of history. I enjoyed the park because a girl with simple beauty gave me a smile that enlivened the day.

> *She works with subtle care,*
> *folds of thoughts twined within her hair.*
> *Smiles as wide as the sky she catches my eye.*
> *She is the star clearing the clouds.*
> ~RAB

The third historic area touched by the trail in Maryland is Washington Monument State Park. The stone obelisk is but seventy feet high but overlooks a large plain from its hilltop. Citizens of nearby Boonesboro erected it in the 1830s as the first monument to the first president.

Tonight, I'm sharing Pine Knob Lean-to with a group of six other through-hikers who started out separately in Georgia but began stay close together, three men and three women with two of the six forming a couple. All hitch over the harder or less interesting sections, which I consider as a valid alternative to hiking every grueling step, the road as well as the ridgecrest.

The Mason-Dixon Line marks the border between Maryland and Pennsylvania. Two British astronomers, Charles Mason and Jeremiah Dixon, who were in America to observe astrological events, surveyed it from 1763 to 1767. As a neutral, educated party, they were asked to arbitrate the dispute over the boundary between the domains of Lord Baltimore and William Penn's heirs. I find it ironic to learn that the line is set with limestone markers imported from England when the land they mark is almost solid limestone. The Appalachian Trail from the Mason-Dixon Line through most of Pennsylvania to the Susquehanna River is within Michaux State Forest, named after a father and son who, like Bartram, were colonial botanists. The trail in this immediate area follows mostly logging roads that wind through pleasant leafy forests. However, most through-hikers dread the trail after Duncannon: razor-sharp rocks turned on edge for sixty miles.

Down the road a few miles lies Gettysburg, a litany of horror in statistics: twenty-eight thousand Confederates killed or wounded, twenty-three thousand Union casualties. Losses were so devastating that soldiers had to be buried in mass pits. Like at Antietam, marble markers crown the high points of cornfields and cow fields, whose soil and stone walls are stained with the blood of fifty thousand men. On one monument, the American eagle flies over all, a carrion bird scavenging over the bodies of men who have accepted war.

Blunders cost the lives of thousands. Sixty percent of General Robert E. Lee's assault force was killed or wounded— more casualties than the entire War of 1812. In a single wheat field, six thousand died, and bodies were stacked like stones in a wall. Men sacrificed themselves. Did they know the price they would pay for one another, for a cause? How long will the chestnut rail fences stand? How long will the stone monuments remain legible? And the men whose monuments to life would have been their children's children, how long for monuments that will never be?

Ironic stories are told concerning events that never should have been, like the Wesley Culp story (from a roadside marker). "Wesley Culp, a Gettysburg boy, spent many childhood days on Culp's Hill, part of his cousin's farm. As a young man, he left home and then joined the Confederate army. His unit, on the way to Pennsylvania, fought a battle in Winchester, Virginia, where Wes found a boyhood friend, Jack Skelly, among the Union casualties. Dying, Jack asked Wes to take a message to his sweetheart in Gettysburg. Wes promised, but carried the message only to his cousin's hill, where it died with him. But it made little difference. Jack's sweetheart, Jenny Wade, was shot while baking bread, the only civilian killed in the battle of Gettysburg."

The sun sets on the remains of 3,512 Union soldiers and 3,320 Confederates interred in unknown graves in the national cemetery. After the battle, the dead were left behind. On July 4, 1863, Lee retreated across the Potomac to northern Virginia. It's spring now, and the fields where so many have fought are contoured into ribbons of old brown and new green. The green signifies hope. It was in the national cemetery on its dedication day that President Abraham Lincoln sought to bind the wounds of the nation in the Gettysburg Address. To quote Robert Orben, "A toast to the weapons of war/May they rust in peace."

Past the road to Gettysburg, the trail travels through Caledonia State Park, once a bustling iron furnace owned by Thaddeus Stevens, the fiery abolitionist. The furnace drew upon twelve thousand acres of hardwood forest for the necessary charcoal. The abandoned pits, used in the conversion of wood into charcoal, can be seen frequently along the trail. The Confederates, under J. E. B. Stuart, burned the furnace on their way to Gettysburg. It was said that the furnace was destroyed not so much for its strategic value, but because of its owner's beliefs.

At Pine Grove Furnace State Park, like at Caledonia, many furnaces are crumbling into decay. Their cauldrons were used to transform hardwood charcoal and iron ore into pig iron. Despite the fact that the stone chimneys are twenty to thirty feet high, trees ten to fifteen feet grow out of their seemingly impenetrable mass. Where does the water come from to nourish the trees? What happens in drought?

The forests seem not to have recovered from the days when they were stripped for charcoal and lumber. Only scrub pines, stunted hardwoods, and underbrush survive on the eroded earth.

Seventeen-year cicadas have emerged after their long sleep in the dark and can be heard in the trailside trees. Despite their name, some broods in the South and Midwest cycle every thirteen years. Although cicadas are the longest lived of any insect, the overwhelming majority of their lives are spent below ground sucking juices from tree roots. The adult phase is but three or four weeks, just long enough to metamorphose, mate, and lay eggs. Colonial red ants often viciously attack the cicadas. The cicadas, uncoordinated fliers, attempt to beat off the attack by buzzing their wings, but they are either unable to fly off or are incapacitated by the ants. The ants, though forced off, come back to renew the fight again and again, attacking the red eyes and posterior. The cicada is vanquished, the ants nourished. Dried cicada carcasses litter the trail, attesting to the effectiveness of the ants as predators.

To pass through the Cumberland Valley, one must do a lot of road walking. The vale is idyllic, barns with overhung haylofts and neatly squared fields, but hiking is painful to the soles and shins. It's hard to accept that this is not a continuous adventure and has its dull stretches. One remembers the peak excitement points of the past and forgets the monotonous straight stretches. He then wonders why the present is not like the oft-remembered high points of the past. The peaks are spectacular, but only because of the plains.

Just as one travels over both valley and peaks on the trail, the Appalachian Trail hiker experiences emotional lows and highs. On some days, one certainly feels like quitting. Isn't five hundred or one thousand miles enough? What more is to be gained from more dirt, wet, and hunger? At other times, one is intoxicated with the wilderness and wouldn't change places with anyone in the world.

A thunderstorm builds over the valley. The red-frame barns and their accompanying houses sit waiting, calm and resolute, like a husband and wife sitting in the hospital room while their child's operation takes place. "Wait and pray," they say, "the clouds will pass."

Outside the shelter, a storm rages. A night softened by rain, hardened by thunder. In a flash of lightning, mountain ridges appear and defining lines from farm fields pave the river valley. Momentary sights are photographed by memory and then examined in the subsequent darkness until the next fissure of light splits the blackened sky bowl. As light cracks the night, foundations of life seem as transitory as the impermanence of the water drops even now rushing to the sea, yet as sure to last as the rain is to fall.

Passed the halfway point at mile 1,024. My shoes are about gone. I've been putting tacks and wires into them for the past five hundred miles. Now the uppers are ripping apart and the soles are separating. I'll try to pick up a new pair in Duncannon tomorrow.

The town of Duncannon on the Susquehanna has class. The buildings are old but stately. The townspeople are friendly to hikers. The river rolls right by the village's edge, dominating the scene here as it does in so many other American towns. Three hundred fifty miles upstream, the Susquehanna begins at Lake Otsego, home of James Fennimore Cooper. The hero of his novels, Natty Bumpo, would have approved of the wilderness concept of the Appalachian Trail.

One of the reasons I hike the trail is to meet the challenges that one constantly faces. For instance, when the soles of my boots broke and the nearest shoe store was a hundred miles away, could I turn cobbler and repair them with wire and tacks? Could I walk with pus and blood blisters on my heels and ankles? At least that is one challenge already met. A present challenge is offered: Can I find shelter before the clouds drop their moisture, and if not, can I withstand a cold, wet night? A future challenge: three days of sharp-edged rocks. And the biggest challenge: Can I walk two thousand miles from Georgia to Maine without much planning, alone? Perhaps through challenges one measures part of his own worth and just as important defines his own limits.

Near the deserted settlement of Yellow Springs, mine tailings are often seen by the trail. Some are from abandoned iron mines, others the result of anthracite removal, detectable by the golden acid streams that flow beside them. The mines remind me of the description of the dark, deep diggings into the earth of the mountains of Mordor.

A woodcock huddles over a downy nestling on the ground beside her. I had passed them both and then seen the chick before the mother flew off. The long pointed bill of the woodcock is well adapted for probing the soil in search of earthworms, the bird's principal prey. If one visits the woods in the late evening hours or on moonlit nights, he may be treated to the spectacle of the male woodcock courtship dance, in which he repeatedly flies straight into the air for perhaps fifty feet then flutters back to the ground. You or I may not be overly impressed, but the female woodcock seems to find it irresistible.

The lean-to is a palace at Rausch Gap, "the Gateway to Saint Anthony's Wilderness." A table has been built around a living tree in the courtyard in front of the shelter. The roof is translucent fiberglass. Running water is delivered to the eating area via wooden ducts. It is by far the best shelter I have encountered.

A female black bear, a cub in tow, approaches to search the shelter until she sees me. She stops to reconsider and then turns back into the woods. In January of her fourth year, a female bear usually gives birth to a single cub, with twins every other year thereafter. At birth, the cubs are about nine inches long, weigh but eight ounces, and are blind and hairless. The cubs nurse during their mother's winter estivation period. (Bears don't truly hibernate because neither metabolic rate nor temperature drops.) After forty days, the cubs cut teeth and open their eyes, and emerge from the den about ninety days after birth, weighing five to eight pounds. The cubs stay close to mom for their first year and follow her omnivorous eating habits. The mother fiercely defends them from all intruders, as more than one tourist has discovered. The protection extends even to the cub's father, who has long since resumed his solitary ways. Male bears have been known to kill their own offspring, which they probably don't recognize. In many minds, the presence or absence of bears, and to a lesser extent deer, serves as a barometer of wilderness. If the deer population is thriving, the land is considered "country." If bears roam, the land is "wild."

As I eat lunch at the Mountain Spring Tavern, two older men at the bar converse in Pennsylvania Dutch, which is actually derived from German (Deutsch). There are many people who have been raised with the language and still speak it. The German heritage is apparent, especially in nomenclature. Der Kessel is a kettle-shaped bowl of hills that the Appalachian Trail passes along. Pever's Ruh (Pilgrim's Rest) is a spring that the Moravian missionaries stopped at on their way westward in 1792. The Moravians, who follow the religious teachings of John Hus, are named for the area of what is now part of Czechoslovakia. They founded Bethlehem, Pennsylvania, on the banks of the Lehigh River in 1794 and soon thereafter sent missionaries to the south and west. The values practiced in their communal settlements are still reflected in their mutual concern for the welfare of the members.

The people in rural Pennsylvania possess interesting faces. The man who owns the tavern is a good example: a nose that twists one way while furrows in his cheeks run the opposite course. One of the German-speaking men has chiseled facial features accented by pure white hair that's combed straight back. Perhaps the rugged facial features can be credited to the ethnic background of the immigrant workers of mines and mills, plus constant exposure to the elements.

Port Clinton derived its name from its position on the Schuylkill River, which later was connected into the canal system. Iron ore and coal came from the mines. Grain, produce, and meat went from the farms to the city. They were all loaded into barges at Port Clinton. The town consists of a grocery store, two churches, a hotel, and maybe four hundred people.

Seven dollars buys a night in a private room with an antique bed at the Port Clinton Hotel. Because it's a turn-of-the-century hotel, there are only two bathrooms for all the guests, which aren't many. The hotel is run by Helen Cavenaugh, who has opened up today despite the death of her husband a week ago of silicosis of the lungs from his mining days. She opens not for profit, but because her permanent boarders, a ninety-year-old lady and three railroad workers, are like family and depend on her.

The patrons of the bar all have thick brogues that sound straight from green Ireland. Pat, the Reading Railroad's superintendent, tells ridiculously false stories of Rommel, Germans, and World War II. A forest-fire warden also bullshits about quarter horses selling for five thousand dollars for dog food and even seriously tells me that he has hiked the trail in South Carolina, a state that the trail doesn't even pass through. The final customers are a man and a woman in their late forties, who had both been married before and are now living together on a farm outside of town.

During the westward expansion, the settlers brought the old names to remind them of home. Port Clinton, Spring Valley, and Yellow Springs are names that were later carried to newfound Ohio towns. Of course, the same thing occurred when British came to America. New England contains hundreds of British names.

Past Port Clinton, the trail climbs to Pinnacle Rock, where the view is spectacular, especially for Pennsylvania. From a high ledge, a one-thousand-foot drop overlooks flatland as far as the eye can see—flat as Kansas, with strip-cropped fields and forest-hatted woodlots. From the Pinnacle, the trail continues for a few miles to Hawk Mountain Sanctuary. At one time, hunters would come up to this mountain, which is on the main migration route for birds of prey, and indiscriminately shoot anything that flies. Today, the mountain serves as a bird sanctuary.

The zinc smelter and mines in the Lehigh Valley at Palmerton have wreaked devastation upon life. The proximal areas have only tree stumps and fallen logs. The outlying areas are but brush and stunted trees that rarely reach twenty feet in height. I heard and saw no mammals or birds except blackbirds.

A few miles past the Lehigh River crossing, an airplane crashed directly on the Appalachian Trail in October 1971. The plane, a Beechcraft 99, cut a swath twenty feet wide and seventy-five feet long across the ridgecrest. If the plane had maintained only a few more feet of elevation, it would have cleared the mountain. Perhaps it was foggy then, as today, but it was a commuter flight from New York City to Allentown and surely must have had an altimeter and other all-weather instruments. Four were killed: the pilot and copilot, a Swiss man, and a man from Allentown. Four lived: a French couple, one Swiss, and a man from Eaton. The plane shattered and burned on impact, but the aluminum construction preserved most of the shell.

Four novices who are hoping to go from here to Maine have sixty-pound packs crammed with nonessentials. After 1.5 miles of easy uphill, they have rested three times. Altogether, they've covered but three miles their first day. I advised them to send much of their equipment home at the Delaware Water Gap, to which they readily agreed, but I doubt they will travel far.

The intensity of bird songs is waning. This drop in sound activity is in conjunction with a decrease in nesting, mating, and territorial activity. Only the whip-poor-wills consistently maintain their calls.

The seventh state, Pennsylvania, and by far the rockiest, is now behind. I welcome the eighth and most densely populated, New Jersey. Until this morning, on the approach to the Water Gap, I had almost forgotten about the importance of this river crossing. For it is along the upper Delaware's banks that I consider my homeland.

The season has turned too far for the shad to be running up the Delaware. When I was a boy living in a dot of a town along the river's upper length, the shad would appear about the same time that green sprouts broke the garden soil. The beautiful fish from the sea would flash in the water, silver scales reflecting in the sun. They were returning to the place of their birth, repeating an ancestral tradition. Their Atlantic Coast range has been considerably reduced from colonial times, when they constituted a major food source, as a result of pollution and the construction of hydro dams. The Delaware's lack of major falls along its lower stretches, however unfortunate for man, has worked to the shad's advantage.

The adults migrate to the headwaters in pairs at night. When their homing instincts tell them that this is the spot, the female lays up to one hundred thousand eggs over a stretch of gravel bed. The male, hovering nearby, quickly releases a snowy cloud of milt over the roe. Most adults soon return to the sea. If they survive, they will return to the river and breed again in later years.

More than a few of the shad had their silver skins marred by sea lamprey scars. This eel-like parasite is actually a fish, whose sucker-like multitoothed mouth attaches to a large fish like the shad. The host fish can be seriously weakened and often dies. Sea lampreys follow a migratory pattern much like that of shad. The adults, free-living at this stage, move up from the sea to freshwater to spawn. Like most other parasites, they outdo their hosts in number of eggs laid, with two hundred thousand or more deposited on the gravelly river bottom. After about ten days, the eggs hatch into larvae and drift downstream to mudflats, where they spend the next three or four years feeding on benthic (bottom dwelling) organisms and then return to the sea. The lamprey's appearance and habits certainly evoke no human sympathy. The large oval mouth, followed by seven dark gill openings, and the two- to three-foot whip-like slimy body arouse only disgust to the human observer. As boys, we would wade the shallow waters with multipronged hooks attached to the ends of fishing poles. These would be used to snag the lampreys through their backs when they were attached to the river rocks. Hauled on to shore and pelted with rocks, the lampreys quickly died, their bodies riddled with fly maggots within a few days.

TRANSITION
NEW JERSEY AND NEW YORK

The Delaware still holds me in her charms.
How I long to be in her arms,
beside the river again.

Love for the multihued eyes of the country,
ever changing, enchanting.
Emerald-eyed forest,
brown-eyed, brown-haired farm earth,
blue-eyed river winking, waving, and smiling
at the boy whose love they have captured.
I have returned to my mistress,
my lover, my inspiration.
When I left,
I thought that I would return
for the love of a woman,
but I return for the love of the land.
I am the long lost prodigal son who has returned.
I am the king who has returned to his kingdom.
I am winter followed by spring.
~RAB

S unfish Pond, set in the hills above the Delaware, is one of the few still bodies of water that the Appalachian Trail has passed. Its clear, cold water sends refreshment into my dirty, sweaty pores. Because of the sharp contrast of color, the lake has jewel-like beauty. The dark-blue water vies with the light-blue sky. The summer green trees hang over the shore at all points except for a few isolated spots where piles of white boulders break through.

Contrary to expectations, the Appalachian Trail in New Jersey has good overlooks of the Delaware and is pleasantly forested. Through the forty miles in New Jersey, the trail successively travels from the Delaware Water Gap National Recreation Area to Worthington State Forest, and finally to High Point State Park. Scarcely fifty miles from New York City are vast stretches of forest. From the mountaintops, one sees only a few signs of habitation. The rest is unbroken forest. It is optimistic that there are still forested enclaves so close to the Eastern metropolitan centers.

At High Point, the trail passes through an extensive stand of forest that burned an estimated ten years ago. The underbrush of ferns and saplings is extensive, while the upper canopy consists only of oaks, whose thick bark has preserved them from fire damage. All other trees—pines, softwoods, and other hardwoods—have succumbed. The oaks even now look the worse for wear with denuded branches and splintered terminal tops, but they have survived and have grown.

Many gypsy moth caterpillars can be seen blowing on their silken strands. Their most serious defoliation, however, will not be apparent until July. The gypsy moths were brought into Massachusetts from Europe in 1869 and have gradually spread westward, causing great damage to the forest foliage as they go.

On this day, the fulcrum point of the solstice,
spring pivots into summer.
The sky's color changes,
from blue to black, from black to blue,
from light to dark, from sun day to moon night.
Counts the rhythmic cadence of time's repeatable flow,
of seasons gone,

of seasons yet to come.
When seasons change, so do I.
Sights once seen are seen again,
filtered by forgetfulness,
purified by timelessness.
~RAB

The season of summer begins. Blankets of heat cover the meadow, capturing the heavy fragrance of field flowers in bloom. Sweat beads dribble down the cheek sides of a meadow explorer. The drone of insects and their persistent attacks demand the walker's constant attention. Fallen petals from flowers make me feel like I'm walking through June snowfields. Fireflies in great numbers momentarily flash over the grass stalks. More fireflies than stars on a clear summer's night. Pinpoints of light amid darkness everlasting. Fireflies with their instant on-off lights make one think that the stars have dropped from the heavens and are twinkling low and near.

Night travel is completely different from daylight travel. A silver-slivered moon shepherds a flock of fleece clouds. Peacefulness is reflected on calm water. But the night also holds its touchy moments. The forest is more threatening, more mysterious, yet more enthralling. At nighttime, the psyche is more aware (somewhat because of fear). One must hike alone in a darkened forest to truly experience this feeling. A great-horned owl hoots from the distance. To the south, another answers. Territorial males, I would think. Barred owls follow with their progressive announcements that sound like "Who cooks for you, who cooks for you." Midnight magic fills the air. I think of the legend of Sleepy Hollow and the headless horseman chasing Ichabod Crane. From out of the dark stillness, deer suddenly break out of the underbrush and gallop down the hillside. The hiker's heart jumps and then recovers calm. Two skunks, attracted by my flashlight, move rapidly toward me. I am forced to darken the light and wait for them to leave. As the flashlight goes back on, the skunks again hurry over to investigate. This game lasts too long, and I scurry away by moonlight. As I traverse through a series of three-story-high boulders known as the "lemon squeezers," an animal flies through the light beam and passes my face. "Bat," cries a Dracula-obsessed mind. But it is only a sparrow roused from its perch.

Time, as well as people, gets lost in the dark. The William Brien Lean-to is no longer in existence, or I have missed it. I must hike to the Fingerboard Lean-to, four and a half miles from where I started at midnight. At 2:45 a.m., I arrive at the shelter, a welcome sight overlooking a moonstruck Lake Tiorati. Canned lasagna serves as a middle-of-the-night snack.

Part of yesterday's (last night's, really) and this morning's walk has been over the first section of the Appalachian Trail that was laid out. It was officially opened on October 7, 1923. It is hard to believe that hikers have covered this trail for more than fifty years.

At Bear Mountain, the trail crosses next to more civilized surroundings, complete with inn, swimming pool, and nature center. The center held a gem, however: a statue of Walt Whitman, my nomination for patron saint of vagabond hikers. The monument, placed by the Harrimans, is a fitting tribute in a fitting place.

> *"Afoot and lighthearted I take to the open road.*
> *Healthy, free, the world before me.*
> *The long brown path leading before me wherever I choose."*

The Hudson River. Somehow, this seemed a goal very long ago. From here on lies New England. I've covered the highest point, Clingman's Dome in the Smokies, and now the lowest at 115 feet. Unfortunately, the only toll on the Appalachian Trail is also here, ten cents to cross Bear Mountain Bridge. It's not the money, just the principle of the fee, that's annoying. I complain to the gatekeeper but still must pay to pass.

Tugboats ply the Hudson, a water highway from the Atlantic to Albany, and from there to Lake Erie via the canal. Train tracks, part of the famed "water level" route to Erie, line both sides of the river. This region is rich in history. Many of the trails follow old mining roads, such as Crooked Road, once used to haul iron ore. Just over the Hudson lies Manitou Mine, where ore was mined during the Revolutionary War and forged into the chains placed across the Hudson to prevent the British from sailing up to Albany. The guard escorting Major Andre, the spy, to his execution, followed this road. To the north lies Continental Village, where the British defeated two thousand regulars in 1777. Most of the hills on the trail were fortified: Fort Hill, Little Fort Hill, Fort Defiance, and Gallows Hill. Proceeding eastward, the trail follows the Old Albany Post Road, where an eroded granite marker reads "54 m to NYC."

The stone walls lining the dirt roadbed stand tall and straight, not disheveled. Despite the walls' age, the stones remain unscattered. The large capstones rest on top, preventing water from seeping into the interstices. Without water, the great wrecker of stone walls, frost, can do no harm.

Landscape may appear static, but it is only a delusion. It changes with the time of the day, the seasons, and the people who live on it. When landscape changes, it is significant and is well noted by the observer. A barn changes color, a tree dies, or a stone wall crumbles. The land, unlike people, changes slowly enough to be comprehended.

My love for the land compares to a man's love for a woman. If I'm ever as sad and as lonely when away from a woman as I am when away from the rivers and hills, I will marry her at once.

Pawling appears as a village out of a Grandma Moses painting, as well it should, because she lived north of here in the Taconics. Old shops, the firehouse, and town hall surround the village square, where I sit and snack on doughnuts and orange juice.

A few miles more of road walking. Thank God when they're finished. The drudgery is lightened slightly by diversions into geographical nomenclature. A small rise to the right is called Purgatory Hill, reflecting Yankee sarcasm in its status as a place "halfway to nowhere." The path skirts around Quaker Hill and adjacent Quaker Lake, named for the Friends who emigrated from New Fairfield, Connecticut, and settled here in the 1750s. Dewey Lane bears a more recent historical epitaph, having earned notoriety by the racket-busting district attorney of Manhattan, governor of New York, and Republican candidate for president in 1948, Thomas E. Dewey. The governor has taken up the role of country squire over his Dapplemere Farm, which is located at the end of the lane.

I welcome the woods again. The last twenty-five miles have been almost exclusively roads, discouraging not only to the soles of the feet, but to the psyche as well. I welcome the steep climbs to the peaks, but a wilderness trail through the suburbs is depressing. Three road walks of twenty-plus miles lie on the trail: the first in northern Virginia after Shenandoah, the second in the Cumberland Valley of Pennsylvania, and the third around Pawling. I rejoice because now this triad of drudgery is behind.

In contrast to the rest of the day, when deer flies and mosquitoes hover constantly, the Wiley Lean-to offers an almost bug-free shelter. I had planned to spend the night here, but with the heat it might be better to do more walking in the cool hours of evening and early morning.

In the twilight, a doe feeds on the lush meadow grass. My whistle draws only passing watchfulness, with her tranquility quickly restored. Much of New York is ideal habitat for the white-tailed deer, for it is a combination of second growth forest and open meadow. A few years ago, outside my home in Cazenovia, New York, I counted more than two hundred deer in less than a two-mile walk after a spring thaw had melted a prolonged snow cover, exposing hillside cornfields.

The white-tailed deer is America's most important game animal. Man has replaced other predators, such as the wolf and bobcat, to keep the deer populations in check. I am not a hunter, but predation of some type seems to be necessary to prevent the herds from overpopulating, resulting in overbrowsing, starvation, and disease. November will mark the rutting season, when antlers will be out of velvet and males begin to joust for territories and harems. It is a common misbelief that the size and number of points on the antlers indicate a buck's age. Rather, they are indications of food conditions. The antlers are lost soon after rutting, in late December or January, and are quickly consumed by rodents. In early spring, the does give birth to one to four fawns. This mother-offspring group is the one commonly seen in summer, sometimes with the addition of the previous year's offspring. The males prefer the solitary life and rejoin the herd in the fall when the cycle commences anew.

The trail crosses Ten Mile River and proceeds through Webatuck, "the land where two streams meet," a gap in the hills that played an important role in the western migration from New England. The Quakers from New Fairfield probably passed through Webatuck on their way to Pawling more than ten generations ago. A spirit of continuity exists between the Quakers and me. On the few occasions when I have attended a meeting, I have been impressed with their mutual concern for one another, reflecting their status as a Society of Friends. Quakers believe that no minister is necessary between God and man and that each man must follow his own conscience rather than strict doctrine. In the late 1700s, my eighth-generation-removed Quaker grandfather, Gerald Ladd, emigrated from Wales. Gerald's grandsons, however, believed fervently enough in the Union cause to fight for it, resulting in the family's dismissal from the Quakers because of the Friends' pacifist tenets.

The trail skirts a lowland bog, complete with hellebore, skunk cabbage, and peat moss. When one thinks of the Eastern mountains, he thinks of stone crags and forested peaks—rarely of swamps and bogs. Yet there are thousands of bogs in New York state alone. Most of the swamps in the northern half of the United States are dominated by boreal forest largely composed of black and red spruce, balsam, tamarack, and alder and such shrubs as Labrador tea, bog rosemary, with its silver-blue leaves, wild cranberries, and bog laurel. The last has leaves that are green above and white below. Sphagnum offers plentiful protection for the larvae of mosquitoes that bog visitors know so well. Because of the acidity of the water, the reptile population of bogs is lower than other wetlands. Usually only bog and water turtles, water snakes, and a few salamanders are seen.

During the last ice age, the range of the boreal forest moved southward, while the Eastern deciduous forest retreated. When the glaciers melted, pockets of boreal forest, such as that near the bogs, remained behind. The cool climate, short growing season, and nutrient-poor, perpetually wet soil prevented the conifers from being outcompeted by the deciduous trees.

THE BERKSHIRES
CONNECTICUT AND MASSACHUSETTS

I want to go and live by the pond, where I shall hear only the wind whispering among the reeds. It will be a success if I shall have left myself behind. But my friends ask what I will do when I get there. Will it not be employment enough to watch the progress of the seasons?
~Journal of Henry David Thoreau
December 24, 1824

On Schaghticoke Mountain, New York gives way to Connecticut and greater New England. Nine states are behind, five ahead. Connecticut is the state of inventors, where more patents are held in proportion to population than any other state. Eli Terry and Seth Thomas gave us the modern clock in 1848. Gail Borden discovered how to condense milk. Isaac Singer invented the sewing machine. Samuel Colt perfected the revolver. John Howe constructed a machine to make pins.

Just past Kent, the trail follows the route that the stage formerly took between Poughkeepsie and Hartford. Stone walls line each side of the road, which, because of erosion, lies deeper than the floor of the woods. When the stage traveled this route, the land was open, cultivated for either crops or forage, but the girth of the trees growing in the cultivated fields of yesteryear give no clue as to their recent return.

With shirt and shorts soaked with sweat since dawn, a chest-high waterfall and reception pool offer great attraction. Removing only shoes and backpack, I take the plunge. Saltwater is replaced by fresh. As I sit upon a throne of rocks under the cascading falls, I feel like a king, only the treasury holds not gold but rather pure mountain water. In the pool, I flow with the current, passing a crayfish in his crevice and minnows on the prowl.

Macedonia State Park ends at Saint John's Ledges, overlooking the Housatonic River. Back in Virginia, a southbound hiker mentioned that all he remembered about Connecticut was cliffs, with the ledges of Saint John's as the steepest. The view is magnificent from the cliff tops. Thoreau said that views of river valleys surrounded by hills are the best. I heartily agree. Forests line the crests, merging into a patchwork quilt of woods and meadows on the hillsides. Below, the river winds in serpentine fashion through the hills, threading a cohesive pattern for the eye to behold.

The ledges didn't hold up to their fearful reputation. Although I wouldn't have liked to be hiking south and had to climb up, the descent involved only a few places where handholds were needed. At the base of the ledges lies an abandoned road that follows north along the Housatonic. The trail parallels this river route for the three miles to Cornwall Bridge. The roadway has deteriorated to the point of uselessness for auto travel because of the roadway's vulnerability to the Housatonic's floods. A clearing on the river's edge offers a good place for bathing and camping for the night. A rock in midriver serves as sundeck for a dust-covered, weary hiker: myself.

After dinner, a flock of ten Canadian geese lands in the river, directly in front of my campsite. After an hour of feeding, a series of honks can be heard overhead and are quickly answered by the flock below. With a loud splash, the new group of six joins the flock, although the two remain separate. Canadian geese mate for life, which can be up to sixty-five years. My Scottish professor called them Gabriel hounds, after the archangel who was the messenger of God to man.

At 4:30 a.m., the day's hike begins under the moon. A mother mallard and her half-dozen almost full-grown offspring search the river waters for breakfast. A little farther on, two deer, shrouded with the morning mist, hear my approach and bound across the river. On the opposite bank, they pause and turn in my direction for a last glance. Then they are once again enveloped in the cloud wisps, and we are separated.

Singing alone along a riverbank is one of the best ways to feel at peace. The words of the song may not rhyme, but the feelings come out. A book of short stories by Joanne Greenburg, called *Summering,* contains one story titled *Singers*, which tells of a woman with The Gift, spontaneous singing that sorts thoughts and emotions into acceptable flows. Like the woman in the story, I once considered myself unique because spontaneous songs helped sort out the workings of my mind, but just as she found, there are many others who do the same.

At 6:30 a.m., the Housatonic is crossed at the settlement of Cornwall Bridge. The houses sleep with shuttered eyes in these early hours. Piles of neatly bundled newspapers lie stacked on the porch of the general store. There is something enchanting about human habitations at rest. From Cornwall Bridge, the trail follows the hemlock-lined Dark Entry Ravine, whose name invokes ominous images of the Grimm Brothers' Schwarzwald. In this case, as in the childhood fairy tales, the threats are more imagined than real. From Dark Entry Ravine, the trail crosses Coltsfoot Mountain, presumably named after the small dandelion-like flower that is commonly found in the eastern hill regions, although the season is too far past for the plant to be in bloom. Indian pipe stem dots the forest floor. The ghostly, almost translucent color is fitting because it is a saprophyte, parasitic on soil fungus.

Cathedral Pines, as the name implies, impresses reverence, humility, and awe onto the visitor, as much as a visit to the cathedrals of Cologne or Notre Dame. Sturdy trunks point ever skyward, supporting a lacy roof of green. Shafts of dusted sunlight, narrowed by fir hemlocks, contrast mightily with the dark forest understory in much the same way that stained glass windows emanate streams of light through the cool darkness of cathedral interiors. Cathedral Pines is owned by the Nature Conservancy, as were Saint John's Ledges. The Nature Conservancy buys pristine property for public trust, with most properties eventually sold to federal or state government units. Cash flow is thus recycled with new areas able to be protected.

A long, hard climb on a hot day leads to the apex of Mohawk Mountain, which has been developed into a ski resort. The cleared ski runs offer sweeping views of the Taconics to the west and Bear Mountain to the north, the highest point in the state and my next goal.

The heat is oppressive. I've been drinking water not by the cup, but by the quart. Still, I fell nauseated. Perhaps I should call it a day, but I'm sure I'll recover in the evening once I've stopped.

At a brook, a girl washes her hair and body. She is a beauty: firm projecting breasts, thin waist, and golden hair framing a serious face. She lifts her eyes, and I am entranced. Loveliness in Connecticut.

A curious monument lies atop Bear Mountain. The man who owned the mountain in the late 1800s built a pyramid of stone on the apex, perhaps two hundred feet high, all by hand. By doing so, he raised the elevation of Bear Mountain slightly above its nearest competitor, making it the highest point in the state. From the top, where only dwarfed trees and shrubs grow, a panoramic view is obtained. How I love the Eastern mountains. If one lives where there's a far view, his whole life seems set right. The places where I have been the happiest, where I have enjoyed and learned about life, have had extended views.

Ahead lies Massachusetts. If Connecticut is the state known for men who invented machines, Massachusetts is the state known for men who invented ideas. William Bradford, Anne Hutchinson, and Roger Williams advanced ideas on community structure and religious freedom. James Otis, John Hancock, and the irascible John Adams led the colonies in independence from Britain, both in thought and action. The orator Daniel Webster attempted to guide the Union through the troubled period that preceded the Civil War. Horace Mann pioneered educational techniques in New Jersey and later in Antioch College in Ohio. Oliver Wendell Holmes still delights the world with his witty writings. One small town in Massachusetts has experienced an incredible concentration of literary talent. From Concord have come Louisa May Alcott, Nathaniel Hawthorne, Ralph Waldo Emerson, and Henry David Thoreau.

At Guilder Pond, I am reminded of my first night on the trail at Springer Mountain. After dinner, I had gone to the western edge of the peak to watch the sunset—rows of color over a horizon of hills. I was alone, and before me lay two thousand miles of wilderness. Tonight, I am alone at the pond, the sun setting, reflections on the water have merged into darkness, and before me lies six hundred miles of wilderness.

> *In night sight*
> *springtime flowers*
> *look like snowflakes*
> *suspended in the air.*
> ~RAB

A weather-beaten, silver-grained barn lends its considerable grace to the meadowland. The vertical cuts of an up-and-down saw date it as a pre-Civil War building. The glass balls on the lightning rods are unbroken, indicating that a lightning bolt has never hit them. The aged, hand-split oak shingles are good for another generation. The broken wheels and a hay wagon in the adjoining pasture reminded me that despite exterior changes, life on a farm is essentially unaltered. The inner qualities that shape a country person's life have remained constant. The farmer is still bound to the land and watches the growth not only of his crops, but also the changes in the trees and the brooks that each season brings. Despite the transformation from mule to tractor and from nights at the hearth to nights watching television, the farmer still belongs to the earth—an earth reckoned from sunrise to sunset, from winter to summer. This contrasts with the city inhabitant, who sets no clock by the sun, no anticipation to the leaf unfurling in the spring.

Pursued by attacking crows, a great-horned owl flies for a safer haven in the dense forest. The crows attack the owl because it raids their nests at night. Up to 60 percent of crow nestlings may be lost in this manner. However, birds make up only a small part of the owl's diet, which consists mostly of rodents, especially mice. It has been estimated that a pair of great horned owls kill more than twenty-five thousand rodents for each square mile of territory. If one considers that a single pair of field mice and their offspring can potentially amount to more than one million in a year if allowed to reproduce unchecked, then the great horned owl plays a role quite beneficial to man.

A pair of owls dominate a territory of about three thousand wooded acres. Both sexes are superbly equipped for the role of predator. With a wingspan of up to sixty inches and talons that have been known to pierce a man's neck and kill him, the offensive weaponry is more than up to the task. The real marvel, however, is the sensitivity of the owl's detection apparatus. The yellow topaz eyes are as large as those of humans, remarkable for an organism of this size, and one hundred times as accurate. The ears, also much more sensitive than man's, play an equally important role in the detection of prey. A blindfolded owl, placed in a completely darkened room with a mouse, will quickly locate and kill the prey. Each time I see one of these giants lumbering in flight in the distance, I am awed by its beauty and its skill.

Across the Massachusetts Pike by elevated walkway. It's a different world down there. I walk and they ride, and that makes all the difference.

The Appalachian Trail in Massachusetts seems to compensate for the lack of standing water in the previous one thousand five hundred miles. Three ponds in just the few miles since the Massachusetts Pike crossing: Finnerty Pond yesterday, with its well-defined shore lined with spruce trees, Anthony Pond, which was formed by a beaver dam, and finally Gore or Lost Pond.

Two brothers from New York City share October Mountain Lean-to with me. Despite having been on the trail for a month, their city influence is still apparent. Each of their packs weighs fifty to sixty pounds, complete with extra shoes, a tent, elaborate cookware, and three weeks of freeze-dried food. Friends bring beer each weekend. With such burdens, they have traveled only one hundred fifty miles in a month. Still, they are attempting to learn about life in the woods, just as I am. It is not as important to learn about the land and what lives on it as it is to love it. With love, the learning comes naturally and eagerly.

A blade of grass in the setting sun displays its stalk of jewels that it has worked so hard to make—seeds that are the purpose of its existence. For the first time in my life, I have lain in the grass and counted as the stars appeared, ever so unsurely, one by one. It is an act of beauty and appreciation. Why have I never done this before? The time seemed so long. One becomes so lost. Yet it was the duration of only a few minutes.

> *The world is all mine to share in*
> *when I see a solitary star.*
> *My hand holds that star,*
> *and touches on its meaning,*
> *then lets it go to be held by others.*
> ~RAB

A field patiently (for time will not be hurried) waits for the trees to cover its nakedness. It is lovely to have hiked through a long stretch of woods and then suddenly break out into a cleared pasture, alone and deserted.

Impaled on a thorn bush in the field are the remains of a field mouse. The hind haunch, legs, and toes are grisly testament to the work of a shrike, which well deserves its other name of "butcher bird."

An uncomfortable night, with rain outside the tent and condensation inside. My sleeping bag was wet through by morning. Up at 5:30 a.m. and over the cobbles at 7:00 a.m. with a good view of Cheshire, a classically beautiful New England town. A monument off Main Street commemorates the Big Cheshire Cheese, which weighed 1,235 pounds, the daily output of the town's dairies, and was presented to President Jefferson in 1801.

At Jone's Nose on Mount Greylock's southern slope, the trail climbs to more than three thousand feet for the first time since Virginia. The angle is steep, but it's good to be on a significant peak again. Mount Greylock is the highest point in the state at 3,491 feet. After traveling most of the morning in the rain, a warm fire and hospitable people at the lodge are a welcome sight. The lodge workers are young, the conversation easy. A girl with a strong voice sings the folk songs of Judy Collins and Joni Mitchell as I drift off into love dreams. One often hikes to be away from fellow humans, but people such as these are worth returning to.

After lunch, families and couples come to the lodge despite the fog. The spell that occurs among those forced to share shelter by the rain is broken, but such moments are always transitory, which serves to only increase the desire to discover and share them.

The clouds break, the sun shines. A breathtaking view is obtained from the top of the Massachusetts War Memorial atop the apex of Greylock. To the north lies row after row of the ridges of the Green Mountains.

ROCK WALLS AND POETS
VERMONT

Maybe he's not a poet man
or
the songs he sings are not complete,
but
he can catch the beauty of patterned leaves
contrasting with a sky of nonpatterned stars.
His mind twinkles with emotion
but
rarely shines.
His words are bittersweet,
waiting for a sign.
~RAB

Across the Hoosic River and over the Cobbles, from which the entire width of Vermont is visible—from New York to New Hampshire. Vermont's nomenclature derives from the French words for green mountain, verd mont. Like Tennessee, Vermont was an independent state in the decade after the Revolutionary War. Vermont also has the distinction of being the only nonborder Union state that was attacked by the Confederates. A band of Rebels crossed the Canadian border and raided the town of Saint Albans. They inflicted minimal damage before slipping back into Canada.

One of Vermont's most famous residents was Robert Frost, farmer and poet. I emphasize both. He spent his first fifty years trying to eke a living from the rocky, infertile soil. He knew about mending walls, tending orchards, clearing fields, and driving cows home. That was his secret as a poet: He lived his words. What better tribute to Frost's home than a quote from his works?

> *The woods are lovely, dark and deep,*
> *but I have miles to go before I sleep,*
> *and miles to go before I sleep.*

Hikers occasionally come across open meadows of thick brushland rather than closed forest. These open areas testify to an agricultural past. Farmers cleared and cultivated marginal land for one or two generations, and then deserted it. Also dividing the forested hillsides are rock walls that have fallen into gentle mounds, their orderliness destroyed by frost, wind, and rabbits, their height diminished by the relative size of the forest and the underbrush of the hedgerow.

Men like my great-grandfather Axe and great-great-grandfather Ladd spent a good portion of their working days building walls that at one time squared off these hillsides. As their descendant, I am free from much of their necessary toil. Instead, I walk the fields and observe the return of plants once cleared away. A colony of white pines rises to dominate the field on the other side of the wall. One pine is twice the size of the rest—probably spared as an ornamental for the originally cleared field. Now its smaller offspring form an ellipse around it, the seeds having favored the windward side.

On the approach to Glastenbury Mountain, I was attacked by a red-tailed hawk. At first, I only heard a "whump" as though something had fallen off my pack. I turned around to pick up the dropped object, but nothing was there. While I was straightening, a blur came in at eye level. The bird then swooped and hit the top of the backpack with her talons. She landed on an overhead branch, glared, and dove at me again.

She employed the same tactics repeatedly: Hit the top of the backpack, glide quickly to my front, bank, and attack again at eye level. My only defense was to hunch underneath my pack and hurry off, yelling, "I'm leaving, hawk. Just leave me alone." The only explanation I can offer for this aggressive behavior is the defense of a nearby nest.

At the top of Glastenbury Mountain stands an abandoned fire tower, which offers a view of wilderness on all sides, more than elsewhere in Vermont, because the Green Mountains spread out more here than in the north. To the south, over Greylock, lightning streaks as a thunderstorm builds.

At the shelter, there was a small midnight disturbance. I awoke to the sound of a broom walking over the floor. A persistent porcupine was gnawing on a shelter post about four inches from my feet. Having prepared for a porky attack, I threw a two-pound rock that landed squarely on the intruder's side and sent him flying.

Arlington is a typical New England mountain town of white houses and steepled churches. Ira and Ethan Allen lived nearby, and the home of the first governor of the state, the Crittenden house, is just outside the town. Stately pines in front of the house are said to have been the inspiration for the Vermont seal. Vermont has the most serene houses of any state I've visited, with the classic colors of white with black trim predominating. Each is a masterpiece set in greenery, yet each is unique. Small towns like Arlington have changed little from when I first remember them a quarter of a century ago. They have neither grown nor shrunk, with outflow equal to inflow. The well-built houses have remained as homes. While city cores rot with decay and suburbs sprout with ugly growths of apartment buildings and shopping malls, the rural small towns of America remain as stable islands in a sea of mobility.

A foundation of an old homestead lingers by the trail, pausing for a few more years until the forest reclaims the land. I am reminded of a long poem of Robert Frost's, a story really, of two distant cousins, the Starks, who have come back to the old hometown in Vermont for a family reunion. They meet by accident near the foundations of the old homestead. The boy enchants the girl with stories of their mutual great-great-grandmother Stark sitting on her rocker on the porch that used to be. She spins stories and gives advice, the last of which is that she hopes her great-great-grandchildren will meet at her homesite on the morrow. The girl agrees.

Not only old foundations speak of ancestors, but also rock walls that divide the wooded hillsides into neat squares. Ancestors who cleared the fields of trees, stumps, and, above all, rocks. Rocks placed neatly into walls. Most of Vermont was agricultural land once. Eighty percent of the state was cleared at one time. Now, it is 80 percent reforested. The men who built the rock walls moved to Ohio, from Ohio to Kansas, their children or grandchildren migrating on to Oregon. Men long dead, survived only by their offspring and their rock walls.

Beavers, never accused of sloth, have by their industriousness made life harder for the hiker. A few years ago, there was only a stream here, beside which the trail followed. When the beavers first came, they cut all the trees up to fifteen inches in diameter, using their front incisor teeth, which grow constantly and need to be worn down. Poplars and aspens are the acclaimed favorites for food, with most hardwoods as intermediate preference and conifers definite dislikes.

When the beavers began construction of a dam, they cut and laid branches with their butt ends downstream. They packed other sticks, rocks, and mud into the webbing until it was watertight. The force of the water held the materials in place. The height and volume of the dam continued to grow because the beavers constantly added wood after stripping and eating the bark. The trail was forced to follow a semicircle around the impoundment, and a boardwalk was constructed to cross the marshy rear. Now the enterprising rodents have constructed additional foot-high embankments around the dam's edges, raising the water level once more. The result is that the new trail is partly submerged, with the boardwalk floating rather than resting on solid ground. My boots are soaked, and I just barely miss falling into the pond completely when the boards upend with the final steps. Still, I'm happy to see the beaver's return to numbers in the Northeastern states as a result of protection and replantation.

Tonight, I pitch my tent beside a musical stream. The day has been cool, a hot meal has lifted the spirits, and many miles are behind me. The gap through the trees offers an awesome view of a long valley with multiple peaks asleep behind it. Horizontal streaks of color outline mountains majestic. My soul can't help but soar when I'm in the mountains.

Bromley Tower offers a grand view on this crisp, clear day. To the south lies Stratton Mountain, with ski trails forming old-age wrinkles down its face.

Dory, the caretaker of Bromley Shelter, and I met on her way out for her weekly day off. Since the nineteen seventies the Green Mountain Club caretakers have been supervising many of the shelters during the summer. They eliminate vandalism and excessive rowdiness, offer help, and pack out litter. All are volunteers whose only income is derived from the dollar fee for overnight use of the shelter.

From the top of Baker Mountain, I rest for a few minutes, entranced with a scene of peak after peak blending the green of the hills with the blue of the horizon. At Lula Tye Shelter, I'm undecided whether to spend the night here alone or down by the pond with the multitude. The pond scene is probably prettier (I'll find out tomorrow), but solitude wins out. Samples from the trail register at Lula Tye Shelter:

"Made my pile of rocks to shoot at the porkies. Hope they stay away. Am very tired."

"North bound hikers. Be prepared with warm clothes for the Whites."

"Deep in the valley, valley so low there came four hikers so damp, so cold freezing their tushes and depressed as hell. DAMN RAIN."

"Green Mountain Mitch and Seven Toes Sylvester writing (Enfield, Connecticut). We're on a five day hike through the rain and pain. Finally a dry tent. I wish I had my guitar. I'd make up a song about how peaceful it is here. Down in the big metropolis of Enfield we don't get much silence."

"I thought that I was free, but I'm one more prisoner of time,
alone, within the boundaries of my mind."
~Jackson Browne

"Joke for the day. Busted my rump getting up to Bromley to see nothing but rain and fog."

A quote reflecting quite a mind for fantasy and an excellent recall of the characters from *Lord of the Rings.* "Stopped by the entwash to visit Treebeard and Quickbeam but no one was here, just us. Shadowfax and I are headed to Bree where I can find the best pipeweed around and stop for the night at Mr. Butterbur's Prancing Pony Inn. I must leave soon, as the Dark Lord is ever present, and his influence will never end. Take care that the Shadow of Mordor doesn't fall over you. Remember that the Age of Man has arrived. It is up to him to cast away and destroy the seven rings and thus destroy the Dark Lord, Sauron, forever. Be at peace and the White Lord will be with you always to guide you along your way."

Little Rock Pond possesses a beautiful combination: a pristine lake in the middle of the Vermont hills and an island in the middle of the lake.

Clarendon Gorge, named after the 1920s governor of Vermont, has a high suspension bridge for the walker to cross the stream, but I choose the low route instead so I can swim. Although the water is cold and refreshing, I'm surprised at the sting when the water contacts open blisters. Creeks and clear rivers hold much more enjoyment than a pool. I can watch the schools of fish near the bottom or crayfish dash into their lairs. When I desire a change of view, I merely push into the channel and float to another location. With streams, the only boundary is the sea.

The Governor Clement Shelter is a three-sided stone structure roughly resembling those in the Smokies and in Shenandoah. It was built in 1929, even before the Appalachian Trail was laid out, making this shelter the oldest of more than two hundred thirty along the trail.

The top of Killington, at 4,241 feet, is the first point where the trail has been above four thousand feet since Shenandoah. How good it is to again be among the clouds, which move in wisps around the stones while the wind howls its complaint to the peak impeding its journey. I can barely see my toes. 'Tis a grand feeling to feel the raw elements: stones, wind, firs, and clouds.

At Cooper Lodge, a few hundred feet below the summit of Killington, I find a temporary haven from the wind, but even here the gray mist smokes through the open windows.

At the foot of Killington lies the Long Trail Lodge, where a hillside boulder comprises one entire side of the dining room. Just past the lodge is the Maine Junction, where the Long Trail proceeds north to the Canadian border. To the east where I will go, the Appalachian Trail leads to Katahdin. Three miles past the junction stands Mountain Meadows Lodge, where by a lake ringed with hills sits an old barn and farmhouse. Both have been converted to house skiers in the winter and hikers in the summer. A small sign offers an irresistible temptation: bed, bath, and breakfast for three dollars. I like the resort's logo, which incorporates the first letters of its name, MML.

On the western peaks, black rolling clouds of a thunderstorm play leapfrog with one another while huge white lightning splits the sky. The rain arrives, at first only as a few big splatters, but soon, to paraphrase Isaiah, in numbers as numerous as the grains of sand in the ocean or stars in the sky.

At Mountain Meadows Lake, I watch a peaceful sunrise from a canoe. Regal colors of gold and blue flow over the hillsides—a painting where the colors change constantly. The change comes slowly, majestically, as night becomes day.

For the next forty miles, the trail leaves the Green Mountain National Forest, crosses private land, and deviates from a straight northern course to an almost due easterly direction. Physical exertion increases because the trek is no longer linear along the ridges but rather traverses them, resulting in a constant up-and-down hike.

The lookout offers a splendid view. To the north lies the long line of the Green Mountains that the Long Trail follows, highlighted by Mount Mansfield. To the northeast stand the Whites, with some of the upper slopes above tree line. I look forward to their alpine vistas.

Rainy, misty hiking, what I call hiking in the clouds. Wet but exhilarating. The open meadows atop Thistle Hill bring to mind the southern balds. As usual, but even more so in the rain, it is good to reach the shelter, where hot soup is sheer delight. I spend the afternoon reading, cuddled in the sleeping bag.

Perhaps the best one-word description of the town of Woodstock is "charming." As a young woman's slight smile and a turn of the eyes It invites the visitor to stay awhilethe village green speaks of New England neatness amid the wayward rumpledness of nature. Once the "common" grazing land of the village, the green now acts as the focal point, the emerald jewel of the town. Radiating like setting points from the green are the church spires: Congregational, Episcopalian, Unitarian, Presbyterian, and Catholic. From the spires, bells made by Paul Revere call the listener's attention to the silence they have just broken. Besides the glory of the churches, there are shops to entrap the traveler with their bait of Vermont maple sugar and cheese, woodcrafts, antiques, and postcards. Many of Woodstock's houses have markings with their dates of construction. Those around the green are the oldest and grandest, reflecting Woodstock's heritage as the onetime state capital and former site of the medical school.

Backpacking forces the hiker to walk the balance line, the edge of the sword, between disciplined deprivation and hedonistic gratification: a tiring, sweat-soaking day ending with a plunge into a cool stream; an arduous, lung-bursting climb followed by a magnificent panoramic view; and the continuous contrast between life on the trail and civilized pleasures—a warm meal, a hot shower, clean, dry clothes. It is by walking this line between sacrifice and satisfaction that one finds fulfillment.

Happy Hill shelter, just six miles from Hanover, is an enclosed cabin with an indoor fireplace. It is a palace. Only one other shelter compares: that in Saint Anthony's Wilderness in Pennsylvania.

Across the Connecticut, the last of the five major river crossings after the Potomac, Susquehanna, Delaware, and Hudson. The Connecticut is an old river, here well before the last glacial movement. It was along its banks, with the use of water power, that America's first industrial towns were founded.

Atlantic salmon, once plentiful in the Connecticut, have been absent for almost two centuries. In 1798, a sixteen-foot-high dam was erected at Turner's Falls, Massachusetts, barring the adult salmon from ascending the Connecticut to their spawning streams in New Hampshire and Vermont. In 1810, the few remaining salmon vanished altogether after other dams were constructed upon the lower river and its tributaries. The increasing industrialization of the Connecticut Valley and the resultant pollution ensured that there were no survivors.

The future of the Atlantic salmon in the Connecticut, however, looks good. With the Clean Water Act, municipal sewage treatment plants have been upgraded while industry has cooperated in pollution abatement. The highland watershed areas in the four states along the river's borders have reforested, decreasing the river's silt load. Fish ladders have been constructed around the power dams, eliminating the obstacles that were the cause of the salmon's original decline in the 1700s. Adult salmon have been imported from New Brunswick to New England fish hatcheries, where the eggs are fertilized and the fry raised. This is a necessary step because salmon, after two to three years feeding in the ocean, return to their home streams to spawn. Atlantic salmon perform this migration twice a year, in spring and fall. Exactly how the salmon manage to find their way through the vast stretches of ocean and then choose the correct header stream is unknown, although ultrasensitive chemoreception of the water may be involved, as well as orientation to the Earth's magnetic field. In the case of the Atlantic salmon, pollution control and human concern for its habitat seem to have paid a dividend.

THE WHITE MOUNTAINS
NEW HAMPSHIRE

Starlight at twilight.
Thoughts illuminated by moon white.
Momentary rainbows of color
at dawn and dusk.
The dawn of birth,
the dusk of death.
Sunsets of myriad color,
followed by twilight.
Sights of pinpoint light,
holes pricked from
lasting ever darkness,
a journey of time
within the present breadth of eternity.
~RAB

New Hampshire is the antithesis of Vermont. One is primarily green mountains, the other is well known for its white stone peaks. They are both triangles, but their points and bases are opposite, such that when wedded they form an almost perfect rectangle.

The state derived its name from the home of John Mason of Hampshire, England, who in 1629 was made sole owner of all the land between the Merrimack and Piscataquis rivers.

Here, as the New Hampshire resident says, "the eye can pleasure itself."

From out of Hanover, home of Dartmouth College, the trail follows rural roads for about three miles. Backcountry roads, unlike modern highways, don't allow you to stop living as you travel them and then resume once you reach your destination. You live with the road and become part of it. You live with the people you walk with, the springs you drink from, the cows you teasingly moo at, and the meadows and swamps you discover bordering the side roads.

Centuries-old sugar maples line the backroads. New Hampshire, like Vermont and upstate New York, is a big maple producer. Despite the age of the industry, its time-honored ways have changed. Come spring, gone will be the beechwood buckets that have been emptied daily. Instead, plastic tubes will conduct sap from the tapped trees, feeding into a larger tube that will drain into a galvanized water trough.

When I travel by the old homesteads of New England, I can't help but yearn for my own mountainside farm. I muse about the opposing philosophies to landownership. If one does not own land, one is freed of the burden of maintaining and improving it. By owning no land, one is free to walk anywhere and enjoy all the earth that one sees. The opposing view argues that owning land is a pleasure. One obtains satisfaction in improving and participating in its development. Ownership of land is security when there is disruption.

Descending on to the fire-colored flowers of joepyeweed, a monarch butterfly delicately folds back its wings, which are boldly patterned in orange-reds and blacks to warn predators that it is nonpalatable. As a caterpillar, the monarch feeds exclusively on milkweed plants, which are laden with cardiac glycoside, a toxin that induces vomiting in avian predators.

With an extendable hose-like proboscis, the butterfly draws up the flower's nectar, a large portion of which will be converted into storage fats. The monarch will need this energy reserve in the autumn when, triggered by lower temperatures and decreasing daylight, it begins its migration to winter in the highlands of central Mexico. On their way south, monarchs often aggregate in the early evening on prominent trees, especially those on the edges of creek or river valleys. A few years ago in Ohio, I chanced on such a tree—a large maple whose green leaves were temporarily covered with thousands of butterflies, gently folding and unfolding their wings.

I watch with satisfaction as the fields in New England return to forest. Many should never have been agriculturalized to begin with because they were too steep and had too little soil cover. After being stripped, burned, and used as marginal land, the fields will return to their rightful place as mixed deciduous-coniferous forest.

Late afternoon lingers in the mountain's summer meadow, when the air hangs in waves of heat. It is a magic moment, for one becomes conscious of sounds that had been present but gone unnoticed: the buzzing of unseen insects, the wind searching a path through the leaves, the brook water dropping over the stones. The setting sun breaks the spell. Fingers of cool wind reach through the heat to caress the face. Sights and sounds retake their normal places, no longer pervading one's entire consciousness. The afternoon changes to evening, when one recalls the extended parts of one's self to again become the whole entity. A time to rest, to reflect, to recall the events of the day.

One by one, the lights of the valley appear, like stars in a rapidly darkening sky.

The fireflies are beginning to decrease in number. No longer do they bring the heavens to earth. I shall no longer confuse the hayfields for the star beds of the universe. I shall miss these sparkles of serenity but will look forward to their arrival every spring.

On the shores of Wachipauka Pond, cattails and reed grass shimmer in the wind. Duckweed, the smallest of the flowering plants, coats the water's surface with uneven green ice. Despite the seeming frailty of the surface water tension, water striders seem unsinkable on their six-legged struts, even when a pebble lands nearby. Below the surface, a tiny stream of jeweled bubbles rises from the leaves of the water plants, returning to the water the oxygen that the aquatic animals have consumed. Amid the rooted plants, boaters propel their oar-like appendages backward in their curious fashion. A giant water bug, great pincers poised in open readiness for unwary prey, lies cryptically suspended in its emerald-leaved lair. Its dark body glistens with a thin plastron, which is primarily nitrogen and acts as a reservoir for exchanging carbon dioxide with the oxygen dissolved in the water. With the aid of this diffusion membrane, the water bug can multiply its diving time, remaining submerged for many hours.

Dragonfly nymphs lurk in the cavernous interstices of *Spirogyra* algae, ready with extendable labia to clamp onto other aquatic insects or even small tadpoles. The nymphs are themselves preyed upon by fish and frogs. If they survive, they and the closely related damselfly nymphs will climb up emergent vegetation and metamorphose into the delicate darning needles that hover above the pond's surface. During their aerial adult phase, the two are easily separated: dragonflies usually have thicker bodies and while at rest hold their wings in a horizontal position, while the thinner-bodied damselflies hold their wings vertically.

The male and female damselflies undergo elaborate contortions during their courtship rituals. The male first transfers sperm from a posterior abdominal segment to a bladder-like pouch near his head. The male and female then twist their bodies into circular loops, with the male grasping the female's head with the tip of his tail as she inserts the tip of her tail into the sperm-containing pouch. After mating, the female will use her ovipositor to pierce the stems of aquatic vegetation, laying her eggs in the slits, or, depending on the species, she may dive under the water and deposit the eggs in sandy shallows. Anywhere from two weeks to nine months later, again depending on the species and environmental conditions, the nymphs will emerge to begin their predatory ways.

In the evening, a lone bullfrog starts his call of "jugo-rum," and a competitive chorus joins in. The male frogs are territorial, each defending his water rights from any newcomers. The females search out the potential suitors, surveying each site and somehow judging such variables as water temperature and the degree of vegetation. These will affect the survival chances of her eggs. Her rounds completed, she makes her choice, although smaller "parasitic" males may lurk on the edges of territories held by the larger males. They rely on the calls of the dominant males to lure the females, with the hope of intercepting and mating with a fertile female before the dominant male discovers her. The parasitic dominant male complex is found not only in bullfrogs but also in field crickets. In both, the chances of success for the parasitic males is small, but without their own territories, it is their only chance for mating until they survive the gauntlet of growth and become large enough to defend their own water rights. High summer now is upon us. The turn of the seasons

> A bloom,
> a full green leaf,
> color's desire,
> white coldness after the fire.
> ~RAB

The smells of the day are accented at sundown, perhaps because of the increase in dampness. The colors also seem brighter. Everything is accented: smells, calmness, insect sounds, one's thoughts. It is the last productive burst before the rest and recuperation of the nighttime.

The motion of water below the bridge transforms reflected starlight into a river of stars to be washed into the sea.

A full moon guides my way through the dark evergreen forest and into the open fields. The landscape oscillates between illumination and shadows depending upon the cloud cover of the moon. Alone in the forest, I find a time of stillness and peace.

Moosilauke is the first place on the Appalachian Trail above timberline. Some claim that the best view of the White Mountains is from the summit of Moosilauke, superior even to Mount Washington's. Before the Civil War, developers built several lodges on the summit for guests to appreciate the vista. The trail follows an old carriage road, now badly eroded, for the last mile to the summit, where boulders from the ruins of the lodges litter the ground. Prior to Moosilauke, the trail crosses within the boundaries of the White Mountain National Forest, the largest area of public land within New England. Within its seven hundred thousand acres, larger than the state of Rhode Island, are forty-six peaks higher than four thousand feet. Fortunately, the government owns 80 percent of the land, a higher percentage than any other Eastern national forest.

New Hampshire was given a momentary reprieve from the lumbering destruction that wracked the country in the nineteenth century, beginning in Maine around 1830. Bangor was the center of the industry, where the state's great white pines fell to the saws of the famed Bangor Tigers. The Tigers worked primarily around rivers and transported the logs by water, but they bypassed the rocky streams of northern New Hampshire in favor of the forests of the northern Midwest—the firs of Michigan and Minnesota—leaving the virgin forests of the White Mountains intact even up to the late 1800s

Men like J. E. Henry knew how to transport the wood by railroad. The lumber barons bought land from the state at scandalous prices—as low as twenty-five cents an acre. They laid standard-gauge railways into the valleys and up the slopes. At first, the plentiful wood powered the railroads. Later models switched to the more efficient coal, which also caused fewer destructive fires. The major problem for the trains wasn't in pulling the heavy loads up the grades but rather in braking the cars on the way down. It was a dangerous occupation with a high injury rate.

From 1875 to 1915, most of the White Mountains were thoroughly stripped. Winter was the peak season, when logs could be dragged over the frozen ground. In summer, most of the camps came to a halt. After the loggers left, the scene was one of utter devastation: splintered stumps, eroded gullies, and twisted, wasted trees. The lumbering reached its peak in 1907, when six hundred fifty million board feet were removed from the state, mostly to feed the nation's construction boom. The industry used very little of the pulp. With the lumber removed, fires swept the area, one in 1886 and one in 1903, with such intense heat that even the soil burned.

It wasn't until 1915 that the Weeks Act created the national forests, including the White Mountain range, to return the devastated land to public ownership. The mountains slowly recovered, although the great hurricane of 1938 caused further destruction. White birch, which is still prevalent in many areas, along with aspen and fire cherry, sprouted in the thin soil. Because their seedlings are relatively intolerant of shade, they are succumbing to yellow birch, maple, and beech, which in turn will give way in all but the low-lying valleys to the original forest of red spruce and balsam fir.

With their sharper, higher peaks, the White Mountains are ninety million years younger than their Vermont relatives, the Green Mountains. Still, at three hundred sixty million years of age, the Whites are about six times as old as the Rockies. The torturous upliftings and folds causing their rise are still evident in the fractured and bent layers of granite and schist. The Whites are appropriately named because ice covers their flanks for half of the year and mica flecks sparkle in the sunlight during the warmer months.

The Appalachian Mountain Club, founded in Boston in 1876, operates a unique system of eight huts, spaced an easy day's hike apart in the Presidential Range of the Whites. From the south, Lonesome Lake Hut, located above Franconia

Notch, is the first one encountered. Mizpah Springs Hut, set in an opening in the boreal forest above Crawford Notch, is the newest, built in 1965. About four and a half miles farther on the Appalachian Trail, all above tree line, lies Lake of the Clouds Hut on Washington's flanks. Accommodating ninety, it is the largest hut.

The huts offer overnight shelter from the harsh environment for a modest charge ($12.00 - $15.75 per person, including dinner and breakfast: 1979 rates). They are constructed of native stone and wood that blend into the natural environment. While they increase accessibility of the alpine regions, they also minimize the effects of overnight visits to preserve the fragile environment, where the harsh weather conditions and ephemeral growing season retard recovery from human intrusion.

Many hikers describe a special feeling that comes from standing on the peaks of the Appalachians. For some, this occurs on Clingman's Dome or Big Bald in the southern section, for others on the Pinnacle or Killington. For most, I believe, it occurs on the barren, windswept twelve miles of trail above tree line over the Presidentials. The feeling is not religious, although similar in intensity, but rather a sense of accomplishment combined with that rare elation of standing on the top of the world.

As one starts to climb up the slopes of the Presidentials, the mixed hardwood forest of beech, maple, and occasional oak becomes interspersed with balsam and red spruce conifers. The hardwood species gradually form into pure stands of mountain ash and white birch. The red spruce is replaced by the black spruce, which is better adapted to the cold constant winds. Soon, even the spruce are gone, replaced by the dwarf birch and alpine willows, none more than two feet high. This point, about four thousand two hundred feet, is the upper limit of commercial timber. The growth pattern of trees gently angles into the horizontal shape that some Europeans call "krummholz," meaning "crooked wood." The kurmmholz's principal component is the balsam fir, *Abies balsamea.* At timberline, the age of the tree trunks rarely exceeds one hundred years, but the root system, protected by the soil cover, may be considerably older. The stunted upright trees and krummholz reach the limit of continuous cover at four thousand eight hundred to five thousand two hundred feet. The elevation at which the tree line ends is largely determined by a combination of wind exposure and winter snow depth. A lack of snow cover results in frozen soil and the desiccation of shoots exposed to the strong winds. Above this line lies the true alpine range. The peaks within the Presidentials can perhaps best be compared to arctic islands within a sea of temperate zone. According to Dr. L. C. Bliss, who has done extensive work on the vegetation of the White Mountains, approximately one hundred species of vascular plants grow above tree line, seventy-five of which are truly alpine. The remaining trees are boreal, that is, most commonly found in forest communities.

The alpine meadows, or alpine gardens as they are often called in the Presidentials, are delightful places—like a bit of the Alps within a few hours of Boston. The vegetation follows distinct patterns. The deep winter snow doesn't melt until June, usually at the protected sites adjacent to clumps of krummholz, extending from timberline to about six thousand one hundred feet. Cranberry heaths *(Vaccinium sp)* and hairgrass *(Deschampsia flexuosa)* dominate, but more boreal herbs are also common. Carpets of the green heart-shaped leaves of wild lily of the valley *(Maianthemum canadens)* are interspersed with the small white flowers and evergreen leaves of goldenthread *(Coptis groenlandica).* The blue fruits of the dogberry *(Clintonia borealis)* vie with the red bunchberries *(Cornus canadensis)* for the title of brightest color. Near springs, the highly poisonous leaves of the false hellibore *(Veratrum viride)* appear as crinkled emerald fans, contrasting with the barren rock-strewn fields. Occasionally seen are the white delicate flowers of *Houstonia caerula* (variation *faxonorum),* a plant endemic to the White Mountains, with the captivating name of Quaker ladies. The snowbank community is the richest floristically, but not as hardy as some of the others. The less protected open areas of the slopes just above timberline are most commonly occupied by a mixture of dwarf shrub heaths *(Vaccinium uliginosum, Ledum groenlandicum)*, Lapland rosebay *(Rhodendron lapponicum)*, rushes *(Juncus trifidus)*, with clumps of mountain sandwort *(Arenaria groenlandica)*, and a scattering of cinquefoil *(Potentilla tridentata)*. The most important species, however, is the sedge, *(Carex bigelowii)*. Almost pure sedge meadows often cover the north and west faces of the tallest peaks. Sedges can be differentiated from the grasses by their triangular cross-section as opposed to the round rod-shaped grasses. *Carex's* dominance on all the higher fog-shrouded peaks is related to its higher photosynthetic efficiency at low-light levels, even in heavy cloud cover. The award for true perseverance, however, goes to the heath, *(Diapensia lapponica)*, which grows in low mats even on the most windswept rocks, optimistically sending forth its white flowers despite the adverse conditions.

Areas too barren to support vascular plants are covered with lichens. All lichens are symbiotic combinations of algae and fungi. The fungi break down the rocks to obtain nutrients and water and act as support and protection for the algae, which carry out photosynthesis, thereby manufacturing food. Lichens are slow-growing but determined. Some colonies are estimated to be more than two thousand years old. More than twenty thousand species have been identified throughout the world. Two of the most common species in the alpine areas of New England are the edible rock-tripe, which usually grow on vertical rock faces, and map lichen on most exposed rocks. Other common species are British soldiers, with their characteristic redcaps, Iceland lichen, ring lichen, and snow lichen.

Including lichens and mosses, the alpine vegetation in the Presidentials and on Mount Katahdin is more closely related to the arctic and alpine communities of the Scottish Highlands, Scandinavia, and the Alps of central Europe than to the Western mountains of America. Even the plants' scientific names attest to their home range—*groenlandica, lapponica, canadensis,* and *borealis.* This relationship has been attributed to the higher moisture levels and fogginess prevalent in the New England mountains as opposed to the drier and sunnier environments of the Rockies and Sierra Nevadas.

On the trail toward Mount Washington, hikers become more aware that the Presidentials are exposed to some of the most vicious and capricious weather known. A large US Forest Service sign warns in no uncertain terms:

STOP

This area has the worst weather in America.

Many have died from exposure, even in the summer.

Turn back now if the weather is bad.

A good portion of the deaths have been "goofers," inexperienced walkers who are inadequately prepared or dressed and die as a result of hypothermia—the sudden lowering of body temperature. From 1849 to 1976, eighty-three people died on Mount Washington. A cross on the western approach, slightly below the summit, marks the final resting place of one hiker caught in a storm. The weather can change within minutes from an eighty-degree summer day at the base to an arctic blizzard raging at the summit. The wind-chill factor is probably the biggest killer. Wind velocity exceeds hurricane force (seventy-five miles per hour) 104 days out of the year. The world record for the highest known wind velocity, 231 mph, was recorded atop Mount Washington in April 1934. The temperature has never been known to exceed seventy-one degrees, and even in the warmest month, July, the average daytime high is only fifty-five degrees. Considering the constant wind and the fact that the summit is encapsulated in clouds 80 percent of the time, the temperatures seem much lower. In contrast to July's heat wave, the mean temperature in January is six degrees with an all-time low of minus fifty-eight degrees recorded. The Mount

Washington Observatory has continuously monitored the weather conditions since its establishment in 1932. The observatory's buildings, like those of the Tip Top House, are bolted into the rocks and anchored by steel cables. In 1968 and 1969, the structures were virtually buried under the snow, with 556 inches falling that winter, seventeen feet in March alone.

When Darby Field traveled from Boston in 1642 to become the first known person to climb Mount Washington, he was venturing into an unknown wilderness, undertaking hardship and risk. Those who climb Mount Washington by any of the fifteen trails that lead to the summit are, in a lesser way, emulating this adventure. Yet, in some ways, attainment of the summit is anticlimactic. A cog railroad, an engineering marvel when completed in 1869, still disgorges its human cargo at the top. The insult is carried further by a road that for more than a century has brought carriages and now automobiles to this unique, once-isolated, fragile environment. More than two hundred thousand people a year now visit the top of Mount Washington. The use of the public domain, with the sides drawn between those who wish to see the land accessible to all versus those who wish to see as much wilderness preserved as possible will continue. To me, the disappointment is immense that the two high points on the trail, Clingman's Dome in the south and Mount Washington in the north, are despoiled with roads and buildings.

Tuckerman's Ravine, a few miles east of Mount Washington, is a prime example of one of the unique geological features of the Presidential Range, the large U-shaped cirque basins known as gulfs. The chute-like troughs such as Tuckerman's and Huntington Ravine and the Great Gulf are about a quarter of a mile wide, more than a mile in length, and one thousand feet deep. Their formation has most commonly been attributed to the erosive glaciers covering this area ten thousand to twelve thousand years ago. Skiers, taking advantage of the late snowmelt, are often present into

June at Tuckerman's, although avalanches are not uncommon. In spring, snow arches are sometimes formed bymelting water running through the snow-packed ravine sometimes forms snow arches. The largest of these was more than two hundred feet long and forty feet high. They offer a challenge to the daring and perhaps foolhardy skier, resulting in at least one death in an attempted crossing.

In the distance, a coyote's cry breaks the stillness of the night. Since the early 1940s, when they first appeared in northern New York and New England, coyotes have been steadily increasing in number. They have accomplished what no other large predator has done: flourish in coexistence with humans, filling the vacuum left with the demise of the mountain lion and wolf. Indeed, the Eastern coyote's darker coat and larger size (fifty pounds or more compared with the twenty to thirty pounds common in the West) indicate some crossbreeding with the Ontario wolf. Despite the alarm of some sportsmen, the coyote's effects on most game species is negligible. The coyote may even be helpful, with its diet consisting primarily of carrion, an occasional rabbit or grouse, and diseased or aged deer.

A gray Canadian jay flits closer and closer to my campsite, ready to live up to its more common name, "camp robber." It is also called whiskey jack from its Indian name, wisskachon or wiskedjak. Although its diet normally consists of insects and berries, it is not above a little stealing, much like the brazen Western jay. It bears none of the bright-blue color of the common jays, but rather is dressed in soft grays, much like the mockingbird, with a white head highlighted in black. The Canadian jay is a staunch resident of the north woods, laying its eggs at the beginning of March, almost as early as the great-horned owl. It is also somewhat of a hoarder, preserving its finds by coating them with saliva and storing them in tree hollows.

SOLITARY FINALE
MAINE

The journey has long since begun
and carries on long after.
I know no joy so deep
as when one man joins his thoughts to another,
when creeks turn to rivers
and rivers flow to seas,
when man is joined to woman,
and both are joined to land.
We are one with each other, one as a whole.
The vastness of thought, the vastness of land
merges with the vastness of the sea.
The vastness of time joins with the vastness of sky.
Against these,
life is infinitely small,
yet perhaps is an infinite part of all.
~RAB

Mahoosuc Notch brings to mind the rigors of the Stekoahs south of the Georgia-North Carolina border. Boulders lie strewn over the landscape, as though a massive stone tower of Babel, built by foolhardy men, had tumbled under the wrath of God. The winter's ice still lies at the bottom of the deeper crevasses, a surrealistic sight in the middle of July. In some stretches, the trail is so narrow and twisting that I have to remove my pack to push ahead. After a morning's struggle, I conquer the first phase of The Notch—a wide vista that opens on to the Sunday River Valley. In the afternoon, the trail still climbs but with less torture.

In every respect matching the rugged ascent of Mahoosuc, the trail descends from Old Speck to Grafton Notch, two thousand six hundred feet in a little more than a mile and a half. Like water, I heed gravity's command and follow ridgetop to valley bottom. My legs feel as though they have been sledgehammered into stone. I can only thank the fates that I'm going down and not up. If I had encountered Old Speck in Georgia, I may have opted for the sweet life and comfort back home.

At one time, the route planners of the Appalachian Trail considered Maine too rugged. Mount Washington was proposed as the northern terminus. But in 1933, a route was prepared using old logging roads. The Civilian Conservation Corps cleared most of the trail, and the last two-mile section was completed on the north slope of Mount Spaulding in 1937.

With the high elevation of the White Mountains and the passing of the season, the reign of the insects seems to have come to an end. Their summer kingdom has been diminished, as has their power over the bodies and minds of men. Even the mosquitoes venture forth only after the sun goes down.

From their fir branch perch, a pair of screech owls watch with unblinking eyes. An old superstition holds that screech owls forebode ill omen. Their long, drawn-out cries, which Thoreau described as "Oh-o-oo-o, that I had never been born," are not indicative of sadness, but are merely the male screech owl's idea of a romantic song.

After a strenuous day, I gratefully make camp at Squirrel Rock Lean-to. The sun hands its ruling scepter of light to the moon and a royal court of stars. The next morning, the sunrise clouds remind me of the lines Homer used to begin many chapters of *The Iliad*: "rosy fingered dawn."

Over the surface of Sabbath Day Pond, a flock of mallards is conducting a food search. The mallard is the chief wild duck of the world, nesting almost anywhere near water that's left unmolested, from city park to millpond to wilderness lake. For such a common bird, the colors are striking: the male with metallic green head and red breast, the female with blue-ribboned wing bands. One of the mallard's habits should be particularly pleasing to the hiker. In its search for aquatic food, the mallard constantly churns the water, drowning mosquito larvae. In this manner, a pond can effectively be cleared of the tormentors.

At Rangely, I fill up on supplies. This will be the last stopover until Monson, a hundred miles to the north. I consider spending the night in the town's country inn, but I feel Katahdin's call now that I am so close. Just a few days more and I will reach "The Great Mountain." A mixture of joy and sadness. I am tempted to follow the example of Harry Thomas, an Indian who has lived on the trail for almost a decade, spending the winters picking up odd jobs in nearby towns.

Wind rocks a colony of white birches. The sorrows of a woman are held within the movements of the tree branches. A mother weeps for her lost children. Tears for her dying husband. Despair over a stillborn child. Or perhaps the tree's movements are from Mother Earth, weeping for her wayward children.

On a deserted beaver pond, a lone pair of black ducks skirt the water's edge. The black is chiefly a New England duck. "If asked to select a game species that most closely resembled in character a New England Yankee," wrote naturalist Hilbert Siegler, "we would choose the black duck. The shy and sagacious bird is the most alert of all ducks. Unlike its close cousin, the company-loving mallard, this independent duck does not generally congregate in immense flocks, but seems to prefer the solitude and company of but a few individuals."

At Saddleback Mountain, the trail once again ascends above the timberline, allowing a view of only trees as far as the eye can see.

Evening at Spaulding Mountain lean-to: A few colors stand guard on the western horizon, reluctant to leave their post against the advance of the stars.

Unfortunately, Sugarloaf Mountain has been developed with a ski lift and gondola. The resort seems out of place in the least developed of the Eastern states. Perhaps I have turned greedy and can tolerate no sharing of the wilderness with the developers.

As I near the end of the trail at Avery Lean-to, some reflection on some of my predecessors seems appropriate. Myron Avery, chairman of the Appalachian Trail Conference from 1931 to 1952, was the first person to cover the entire trail. Starting in the 1920s, he blazed many of the original sections, including parts of his home state of Maine. In 1936, he completed his final section in Virginia.

Earl Schaffer was the first person to hike the trail in a continuous ribbon, quite a feat in 1948, when the conditions were more primitive. Seventeen years later, when he was forty-five, he hiked the trail in the opposite direction, starting in Maine. Earl died in 2002, but his comparison of the first and later hikes make an interesting narration.

Perhaps the most famous of all Appalachian Trail hikers has been Grandma Gatewood. At the age of sixty-seven, she became the first woman to hike the trail continuously. She did it alone, with a duffle bag, a raincoat, a couple of days' worth of food, and little else. People who live along the trail still tell of meeting Emma Gatewood, or of putting her up for the night, as proudly as if George Washington has slept in their homes. This spirited lady from Ohio died in 1973 at age 85.

As of 1977, more than 181 hikers had completed the trail in a single year, including Frederick Leahring, who completed the trail in 1963 at the age of eighty-two. The exact number is unknown because some never report. Before the early 1970s, the Appalachian Trail Conference attempted to keep scrupulous records, verifying who completed the entire trail, but eventually abandoned that practice. Hiking the Appalachian Trail should offer a challenge, but the challenge lies within the hiker—not in an award or record.

Others besides Earl have hiked the trail twice. Chuck Ebersole covered the trail the first time with his son Johnny and their "beagle dog with pack, Snuffy," and later rehiked the trail alone. Dorothy Laker has hiked the entire trail three times. I don't think I would like to follow their example; I have no desire to walk the roads of New York and Virginia again. Perhaps I would like to linger a bit at places that have lured with siren songs: Laurel Falls in Tennessee, Baker Peak in Vermont, the lonely lakes of Maine, and, of course, Cades Cove and the surrounding balds, which offer harmony and exhilaration.

In Maine, some of the original trail markers are still visible. The markers are almost entirely absent from the rest of the trail. Constructed of galvanized steel, the four-inch diamond markers bear the Appalachian Trail insignia and the legend "Appalachian Trail—Maine to Georgia."

With greased-back heads and arrayed in gaudy colors, wood ducks seem to be the epitomy of 1950s teenagers on the wing. A pair of these wild juvenile delinquents, the male marked by a white eye ring, cavort in the middle of their favorite playground—an abandoned beaver pond. Their preference for nesting in hollow trees near the water ties their success with that of the beaver, whose dams provide the required habitat. With the beaver's near extinction before World War II, the wood duck's numbers were drastically reduced. The cause of this demise, man, also came to the wood duck's assistance by providing wooden boxes as substitutes for dead trees. Unfortunately, a number of predators, including raccoons, looked to the boxes as prime sources of fresh eggs. An inverted metal funnel fastened to the supporting post discourages this practice to some extent. As with most other birds, the wood duck's juvenile period is the time of greatest danger. Mortality can occur at the egg stage from predation by raccoons, snakes, and rodents. Subsequent to hatching, the chicks must transit from the nest to the open water, with foxes, dogs, hawks, and weasels liking nothing better than a tasty bit of fluff for lunch. Even in the relative safety of the water, the ducklings can fall prey to hawks, larger fish such as pike and bass, and especially snapping turtles.

Twilight at Pierce Pond
A fingernail moon floats above
a sunset sky of crowded colors
~RAB

The guidebook warns that reservations for boat crossings of the Kennebec River must be made far in advance. With forty inches of rain falling annually in Maine, the river is constantly full and is made even more treacherous by a paper company's dam upstream that unpredictably releases water to flush logs down to the pulp mills. I have heard that the river is fordable, barring heavy rains, or dam releases, two hundred yards upstream from the boat crossing. Despite the heat, the water is ankle aching cold. I have to remove my pack and float it in the water to cross. Slippery algae coats the rocks, and I have no desire to follow the fate of a hiker in New Hampshire who attempted to ford a flooded stream while wearing her heavy pack. She slipped, was pulled under the water, and drowned. What made the incident even more tragic was that her brother tried to help but was also killed.

As the waves wash over me I realize how fatigued I am. My legs initially refuse to kick but faced with the prospect of being swept into the lake I kick and swim with all that is left. With relief from fear and the numbing water, I reach the north side. The last four treacherous stretches of the trail are now behind me: the twisted, wrecked footbridges of Laurel Gorge, the twelve and a half miles of the trail above tree line in the Presidentials, Mahoosuc Notch-Old Speck, and the crossing of the Kennebec.

From Moxie Bald, Katahdin stands as a beacon to the north, only sixty miles by air but more than 130 by trail. In another week, I hope to be on its peak.

The trail passes through stands of almost pure-white pines, the tree that identifies Maine with tall masts and shipbuilding. It is the dominant tree for most of Maine, although spruce is widespread in the far northern and coastal regions. The white pine is the largest tree in the state and has among the longest life spans—up to two hundred fifty years—exceeded only by the hemlock.

Under the warm summer moonlight, I decide to hike on to Old Stage Road Lean-to, but after a mile, clouds quickly cover the moon and the raindrops descend. There is only darkness. Wetness through clothes, coldness penetrating to the core. Aloneness. Fear. Shadows transformed by imagination into abysses brimming with danger. Fighting panic and then calm—the realization of the power, the beauty, and the call of nature at nighttime. The next morn, the sky is clear:

> *Dawn arises,*
> *dawn exposes*
> *her golden gift of light.*
> ~RAB

Near the Carry Ponds, the trail crosses by (or perhaps through would be more accurate) a peat filled bog which started as a glacial gouge ten thousand to twelve thousand years ago. The original deep pond was slowly filled with layers of organic debris. The cold climate and the anaerobic conditions at the bottom of the pond slowed decomposition, creating favorable conditions for the accumulation of peat. As a rough rule, one foot of peat forms every five hundred years. Acid bogs, such as this one, are characterized by a shoreline vegetation of black spruce, leatherleaf, blueberry, cranberry and Labrador tea, easy to identify because of the thick brown fuzz coating the underside of its leaves. Floating mats of sphagnum moss extend into the open water. Although quaking underfoot, the carpet on the water is strong enough to support the weight of a person. On the shore, tamarack and spruce trees grow out of the sphagnum. Despite their twelve- to fifteen-inch height, their age may exceed one hundred years. The acidic and nutrient-poor water stunt the trees' growth. Bog waters are low in nitrogen, potassium, and phosphorus because these elements are tied up in the peat. Although they aren't present in this particular bog, insectivores such as the sundew and pitcher plants frequently grow along the bog's edge. They are able to extract some of the scarce nutrient requirements from the bodies of insects, a switch from the usual herbivore-plant interaction.

Although just twelve corporations hold 52 percent of the land in Maine, the trail is fairly well protected thanks to the cooperation of the paper companies. It is in the Mid-Atlantic states, where the public ownership is at its least, that the trail needs the most assistance. An amendment to the National Scenic Trails System Act authorizes, but has not yet appropriated, ninety million dollars over the next three years to create a permanently protected corridor for the Appalachian Trail. The intent is to ensure that up to 125 acres per mile along the trail remain undeveloped. This will particularly pertain to the six hundred miles of the Appalachian Trail that cross private land and especially to the one hundred eighty miles of roadway. The trail in these sections will be rerouted, and the new route will be protected by either scenic easements, land acquisition, or, as a last resort, through land condemnation. Planners will try to route the trail along boundary lines, although this will be impossible in some places. The areas that are deemed most critical and of the highest priority are northern Virginia and West Virginia near Harpers Ferry, Shenandoah Mountain in New York, and the Poconos and Wolf Rocks in Pennsylvania. The entire trail will never be as pristine as the two hundred fifty miles in Maine, but the right-of-way must be preserved from further development. Where developed, alternate routes must be found.

A moose, his head streaming with water runoff, ceases feeding off the marsh bottom. I freeze, and with adrenalin pumping through the bloodstream, look for a nearby stout tree to climb. The fear is probably groundless. Although stories abound of a moose attacking a human, they are more myth than fact. Still, when a one-thousand-five-hundred-pound animal gives you the eye, and his antler rack alone probably weighs more than you do, it's a good idea to have a contingency plan. This old fellow soon resumes his browsing, searching for the fifty pounds of vegetation he requires each day. I am guessing that this one is a male because the bulls prefer to roam alone during all but the rutting season. He is too large to be a juvenile, and a female would probably have a calf nearby. In her third year, a female moose gives birth to a single calf, sometimes twins. As with most other large animals, the moose's reproductive potential is low. One-half of the females don't give birth each year. As the tallest animal in the Americas, and second only in weight to the bison, predatory mortality is almost nil in Maine (disregarding man), although wolves take their toll in the West. Some offspring are lost to disease, starvation, or drowning, but with a little luck, a moose can live to the ripe old age of twenty. Like many of the New England ducks, the moose has prospered with the resurgence of the beaver, whose ponds provide the aquatic vegetation for food.

In an opening by Chairback Gap Lean-to, the day is brought to a close. The smells are accented at sundown, perhaps because of the increase in dampness. The colors are brighter, and the calmness, insect sounds, and thoughts are more pronounced. It is the last productive burst before the peaceful night.

A spruce grouse crouches under a tamarack, momentarily delaying its decision to flee. The spruce grouse resembles the ruffed except that its tail is black tipped with russet, there is a red patch above the eye, and the body is more grayish than the reddish brown of the ruffed grouse. Although the spruce grouse's flesh is reportedly unpalatable because the bird's diet consists primarily of resin-laden spruce and fir forage, overhunting has eliminated it from much of its former range. Its tame ways and trust of man make it an easy shot. During winter, the toes of the spruce grouse, like the ruffed, are lined with rows of small rods, which act as snowshoes and are shed in the spring.

One could do much worse than be a chronicler of sunrises and sunsets. With such occupation, there is assurance that time has been well spent.

I write for as long as the candle burns, but eventually the flame must die.

A Reluctant Atheist's Outlook on Death
In the mid of the night,
it's a lonely sight
to see an airplane light
blend into the horizon.
~RAB

I value writing above all other forms of expression because it lasts. It has permanence. It can be passed on from person to person, generation to generation, century to century. Other forms of expression—a touch, a thought, a song, a warm kiss—are transitory. Writing comes closest to eternal expression, that is, outside time's boundaries. Plato's writings are as easily read today as they were two thousand five hundred years ago. For the solitary person, writing is also the best compromise. One is alone, the necessary prerequisite for thought and observation, but one is also able to communicate with others when the writings are read.

The most promising situation for creativity, the inspiration of an idea, is nonstructure. Nonstructure is freedom for traveling, watching sunsets, or exploring woods. Yet the most promising situation for productivity, or the accomplishment of the creative idea as with writing, is structure—scheduled time when one disciplines the self to work, to produce. For the initiation of the idea, freedom is needed, but for its production, structure is needed.

One of the prime dangers in writing is becoming too caught up in your own wares. A full moon behind laurel trees, rows of ruby-rubbed clouds in the western sky, or lightning streaks splitting the sky bowl become only flashes of opportunity to put pen to paper. A fine love becomes only inspiration for poetry. One forgets to just watch, to feel, and to appreciate rather than search for the inspiration to write. Sometimes it is better to be caught unaware and drawn into the momentum of the moment.

A loon silently cuts a V into the surface of Rainbow Lake. Loons are excellent divers, usually submerging for less than a minute in pursuit of underwater prey, although they can stay below the surface for more than ten minutes. Loons seem to flourish only with the solitude of the northern, fir-lined lakes. The strange, haunting laugh of the loon reminds me of Edward Forbush's statement that "loons typify the stark wilderness of primeval nature."

A majestic tree holds court from its throne, separated from its subjects that crowd the stream bank. Its lineage is proved by its royal crown, with stars for jewels.

Governor Percival D. Baxter gave Baxter State Park, centered around Mount Katahdin, to the people of Maine. A bronze marker at Katahdin Stream Campground recalls the governor's statement: "Man is born to die, his works are short lived, buildings crumble, monuments decay, wealth vanishes. But Katahdin in all its glory forever shall remain the mountain of the people of Maine."

Part of Katahdin's beauty is that it is a monadnock, an isolated mountain surrounded by plain. This is reflected in one of the translations of its Indian name: "He Who Stands Alone." Although more than a day's hike from here, the mountain lies silhouetted against the evening sky. I am reminded of Thoreau's writings about the night before he reached Katahdin in 1846. Awakened by a dream, he arose before dawn. "There stood Katahdin with distinct and cloudless outlines in the moonlight, the rippling of the rapids was the only sound to break the stillness."

From the campground, it is an eight- to ten-hour round-trip hike to the apex of Katahdin, a climb of four thousand feet in five miles. The trip can be treacherous on any but the clearest days. Even now, the clouds hide the summit. I hope my luck holds better than some others, such as Elmer Onstet, who hiked the entire trail to arrive in Maine in October, only to be unable to climb Katahdin because of hazardous weather conditions. Thoreau said that the god Pamola is always angry with those who climb to the summit of Katahdin. "The tops of the mountains are unfinished parts of the globe...Simple races, as savages, do not climb mountains—their tops are sacred and mysterious tracts never visited by them." This final section of the Appalachian Trail climbing Katahdin's slope, the Abol Trail, passes by Thoreau Spring. It is fitting that the trail ends with a reminder of Thoreau, for he, above all, knew and loved the wild areas.

After more than one hundred days walking the mountaintops, I reach my goal. The sign atop Katahdin says it all:

BAXTER PEAK ELEVATION 5,267
NORTHERN TERMINUS OF THE APPALACHIAN TRAIL
A MOUNTAIN FOOTPATH EXTENDING
2,024 MILES TO SPRINGER MOUNTAIN, GEORGIA

As Aldo Leopold stated in his preface to *Sand County Almanac*, "There are some who can live without wild things and some who cannot." I am among those who cannot.

BIBLIOGRAPHY

Appalachian Mountain Club. *AMC Field Guide to Mountain Flowers of New England.* Boston: Appalachian Mountain Club Inc., 1977.

Appalachian Trail Conference. *Guide to the Appalachian Trail in Central and Southwestern Virginia.* Harpers Ferry, West Virginia: Appalachian Trail Conference Inc., 1974.

Appalachian Trail Conference. *Guide to the Appalachian Trail in Massachusetts and Connecticut.* Harper's Ferry, West Virginia: Appalachian Trail Conference Inc., 1972.

Appalachian Trail Conference. *Guide to the Appalachian Trail in New Hampshire and Vermont.* Harper's Ferry, West Virginia: Appalachian Trail Conference Inc., 1968.

Appalachian Trail Conference. *Guide to the Appalachian Trail in Tennessee and North Carolina.* Harper's Ferry, West Virginia: Appalachian Trail Conference Inc., 1973.

Belcher, C. Francis. "The Logging Railroads of the White Mountains." *Appalachia,* (1959), 517-529.

Bliss, L. C. "Alpine Plant Communities of the Presidential Range, New Hampshire." *Ecology,* 44 (1963), 678-697.

Brewer, Carson. *Hiking in the Great Smokies.* Knoxville, Tennessee: Holston Printing Co., 1962.

Brockman, C. Frank. *Trees of North America.* New York: Golden Press, 1968.

Caras, Roger. *North American Mammals.* New York: Meredith Press, 1967.

Coolidge, P. T. *History of the Maine Woods.* Bangor, Maine: Furbish-Roberts Printing Co., 1963.

Dillard, Annie. *Pilgrim at Tinker Creek.* New York: Harper's Magazine Press, 1974.

Doolittle, Jerome. *The Southern Appalachians.* New York: Time-Life Books, 1975.

Ellman, Richard and Robert O'Clair (Eds.). *The Norton Anthology of Modern Poetry.* New York: W. W. Norton, 1973.

Fisher, Ronald. *The Appalachian Trail.* Washington, DC: National Geographic Society, 1972.

Frome, Michael. *Strangers in High Places: Story of the Great Smoky Mountains.* Garden City, New York: Doubleday, 1966.

Frost, Robert. *Selected Poems of Robert Frost.* New York: Holt, Rinehart and Winston, 1963.

Garvey, Edward. *Appalachian Hiker: Adventure of a Lifetime.* Oakton, Virginia: Appalachian Books, 1971.

Greenburg, Joanne. *Summering.* New York: Avon Books, 1974.

Harper, Francis. *The Travels of William Bartram, Naturalist's Edition.* New Haven, Connecticut: Yale Univ. Press, 1958.

Hesse, Herman. *Gertrude.* London: Vision Press, 1955.

Kephart, Horace. *Our Southern Highlands.* New York: MacMillan, 1913.

Leopold, Aldo. *A Sand County Almanac.* Oxford: Oxford Univ. Press, 1949.

New York, New Jersey Trail Conference. *Guide to the Appalachian Trail in New York and New Jersey.* New York: Walker and Co., 1972.

Niering, William. *The Life of the Marsh: The North American Wetlands.* New York: McGraw-Hill, 1966.

Ogburn, Charlton. *The Southern Appalachians: A Wilderness Quest.* New York: William Morrow, 1975.

Porter, Eliot and Edward Abbey. *Appalachian Wilderness: The Great Smoky Mountains.* New York: Ballantine Books, 1973.

Potomac Appalachian Trail Conference. *Guide to the Appalachian Trail and Side Trails in the Shenandoah*

National Park. Washington, DC, Potomac Appalachian Trail Club Inc., 1974.

Potomac Appalachian Trail Conference. *Guide to the Appalachian Trail from the Susquehanna River to Shenandoah National Park*. Washington, DC: Potomac Appalachian Trail Club Inc., 1974.

Rickett, Harold. *Wild Flowers of the United States, Vol. 1. The Northeastern States*. New York: McGraw-Hill, 1965.

Rickett, Harold. *Wild Flowers of the United States, Vol. 2. The Southeastern States*. New York: McGraw-Hill, 1967.

Robbins, Chandler, Bertel Brunn, and Herbert Zim. *Birds of North America*. New York: Golden Press, 1966.

Sherman, Steve and Julia Older. *Appalachian Odyssey: Walking the Trail from Georgia to Maine*. Brattleboro, Vermont: Stephen Greene Press, 1977.

Shields, A. Randolf. *The Cades Cove Story*. Gatlinburg, Tennessee: Great Smoky Mountains Natural History Association, 1977.

Siegler, Hilbert. *New Hampshire Nature Notes*. Oxford, New Hampshire: Equity Publishing Co., 1962.

Smith, Robert. *Ecology and Field Biology*. New York: Harper and Row, 1966.

Solzhenitsyn, Aleksandr. *One Day in the Life of Ivan Denisovich*. New York: Bantam Books, 1963.

Sutton, Ann and Myron Sutton. *The Appalachian Trail: Wilderness on the Doorstep*. Philadelphia: J. B. Lippincott, 1967.

Tanner, Ogden. *New England Wilds*. New York: Time-Life Books, 1974.

Thomas, Bill. *The Swamp*. New York: W. W. Norton, 1976.

Thoreau, Henry. *The Maine Woods, in: The Writings of Henry David Thoreau, Walden Edition*. Boston: Houghton-Mifflin, 1906.

Whitman, Walt. *Complete Poetry and Selected Prose*. (James E. Miller Jr., Ed.) Boston: Houghton-Mifflin, 1959.

ABOUT THE AUTHOR

Robert Browne is a professor of ecology at Wake Forest University and for many years directed the Wake Forest University Environmental Porgram.

He has conducted research in twenty-six countries, most in the Mediterannean basin, Ecuador and Peru and teaches an ecology course during the summers in Australia. His first love, and the focus of many research projects, is the Appalachian Mountains.

Although not as extensive as the Appalachian Trail, he has completed the Long Trail in Vermont and enjoyed walking the lengths of two of Britain's better known long-distance footpaths, the Cumbrian Way and the Dale's Way. In the summer of 2015, he walked from his home in Winston-Salem, NC to the Appalachian Trail on Mt. Rogers, VA.

The author of more than 70 scientific papers, he has also written a work of fiction, *Three Steps from Heaven*.

Printed in Great Britain
by Amazon